T0323743

Travel

Steve Shipside

- Fast track route to getting the most out of your travelling

- Covers all the key techniques for savvy travelling, from getting competitive rates from hotels and maximising air miles, to staying healthy and keeping on top of expenses

- Lessons and tips from some of the world's great travel successes, such as European Low Cost Airlines and the TGV, and ideas from smart travellers about ecotourism, adventure travel and retro travel

- Includes a glossary of key concepts and a comprehensive resources guide

>>EXPRESS EXEC.COM<<
essential management thinking at your fingertips

LIFE & WORK

10.04

First published 2002 by
Capstone Publishing (a Wiley company)
8 Newtec Place
Magdalen Road
Oxford OX4 1RE
United Kingdom
http://www.capstoneideas.com

CIP catalogue records for this book are available from the British Library and the US Library of Congress

ISBN 1-84112-198-3

This book is printed on acid-free paper

Substantial discounts on bulk quantities of Capstone books are available to corporations, professional associations and other organizations. Please contact Capstone for more details on +44 (0)1865 798 623 or (fax) +44 (0)1865 240 941 or (e-mail) info@wiley-capstone.co.uk

Contents

Introduction to ExpressExec

ExpressExec is 3 million words of the latest management thinking compiled into 10 modules. Each module contains 10 individual titles forming a comprehensive resource of current business practice written by leading practitioners in their field. From brand management to balanced scorecard, ExpressExec enables you to grasp the key concepts behind each subject and implement the theory immediately. Each of the 100 titles is available in print and electronic formats.

Through the ExpressExec.com Website you will discover that you can access the complete resource in a number of ways:

» printed books or e-books;
» e-content – PDF or XML (for licensed syndication) adding value to an intranet or Internet site;
» a corporate e-learning/knowledge management solution providing a cost-effective platform for developing skills and sharing knowledge within an organization;
» bespoke delivery – tailored solutions to solve your need.

Why not visit www.expressexec.com and register for free key management briefings, a monthly newsletter and interactive skills checklists. Share your ideas about ExpressExec and your thoughts about business today.

Please contact elound@wiley-capstone.co.uk for more information.

Introduction to Travel

» Once the preserve of the privileged, travel is now available to all.
» Travel and tourism is a huge industry, and expanding.
» There is a wide choice of levels of cost, destination and content.

"I cannot rest from travel; I will drink
Life to the lees."

Alfred (Lord) Tennyson, Ulysses

Travel, so they say, broadens the mind, enhances cultural awareness, and brings nations together typifying the very best element of globalization. This is a little hard to square with the era of mass tourism and packaged holidays. It's hard to see just how an organized outing to a Disney theme park falls into the category of "drinking life to the lees." The seaways of Ulysses' soul-searching epic voyage are patrolled by cruise liners and littered with floating air mattresses. The culturally elevating grand tour of Tennyson's era is now a trail of tour buses and ice cream vendors. On the other hand, travel in the time of Tennyson was very much the preserve of the privileged. Voyages like the Odyssey came but once in a heroic age, while today even Homer Simpson could manage to make it to the Mediterranean.

Travel is now within the reach of all – so much so, some would say, that it has become a commodity, devoid of romance. It has certainly become big business, being the world's fastest growing industry and one with an extraordinary amount of impact. The World Travel and Tourism Council (WTTC), a global forum for evaluating the full economic impact of travel and tourism, predicts that by 2011 the travel and tourism economy will constitute 11% of global GDP (see Chapter 5, The Global Dimension). It will soon be responsible for more than a tenth of the world's jobs.

The globalization of commerce makes it ever more likely that we will find ourselves crossing borders for business, while a dramatic decrease in pricing and an increase in travel ambitions mean that we are all likely to take our vacations in places of which a previous generation would barely have heard. Those who bemoan the impossibility of trailblazing travel would do well to note the case of Dennis Tito, the first fare-paying passenger in space, and the forthcoming attractions of low-orbit and high-atmosphere voyages (see Chapter 6, The State of the Art).

The mass market may have dimmed the romance and turned travel into a commodity, but in the process it has made travel cheaper than ever (see Chapter 7, In Practice: Travel Success Stories). At the same time, the reaction to packaged tourism means that ecotravel and ecotourism have never been more popular among those globetrotters who have as much concern for the globe as for the trotting (see Chapter 8, Key Concepts). Meanwhile, the Express Exec trying to get the most from that business trip has never had a wider choice of luxury, lifestyle, perks, or budget options to oil the wheels of industry (see Chapter 10, Ten Steps to Making Travel Work).

Travel as a business is expanding fast, but it is expanding in all directions. Where once travelers were separated into First, Business, or Economy, they can now explore categories from elite to eco-sensitive, business to broke, athletic to apathetic. Whatever you want is out there; all you have to do now is decide who you are.

What is Travel?

» Splashing out versus saving on flights
» Space travel (Dennis Tito) versus Time travel (cruise ships and Zeppelins)
» Travelers versus Tourists
» Adventure versus Ecotourism.

Leaving aside the obvious about A-to-B and wheels versus wings, the defining development of travel today is that the sheer volume of travelers, combined with the extraordinary amount of choice in terms of how to travel, means that there is a lot more to travel than simply getting somewhere. Now more than ever, most forms of travel involve a certain degree of self-definition – travelers have to decide just what kind of experience they want, or what kind of people they want to be for the duration of the journey.

Only an airline could get away with the blunt assertion that *homo traveler* comes in no more than three varieties (First, Business, and Economy). The most casual glance around any airplane will instantly show that the distinction is misleading. The back end of an airplane is as full of people traveling to make their living as the front end is full of business people taking it easy and living it up. The difference in pricing on airplane seats alone can mean that a full-fare, front-of-plane passenger is spending ten times as much as a more parsimonious fellow-passenger seated somewhat nearer the tail fin. Of course, more often than not the "choice" in that case comes down to whether the individual or the company is paying; but even then there is a surprising degree of personal choice, otherwise the frequent-flyer program (FFP) would never have been invented. FFPs are an elegant form of bribery, and like most forms of bribery are intended to ensure that individuals do something they would otherwise not have done – in this case, stay loyal to one airline. To cynics, the very existence of FFPs is proof that there are better deals to be done on other airlines. Indeed, the advent of no-frills airlines (see Chapter 7, In Practice: Travel Success Stories) shows that even business flyers are prepared to forgo their Air Miles, along with seat numbers and individual non-dairy creamer sachets, when the alternative is cheap, no-fuss flying.

A growing number of business people are eschewing the airplane altogether in favor of the new generation of high-speed trains that may have similar total journey times, but that allow a traveler to spend more of that time seated in front of a table on which a laptop actually fits (Chapter 7, In Practice: Travel Success Stories). Even the hub system, the backbone of US and transatlantic flying, is being challenged by the advent of newer airlines, smaller regional airports, and Boeing's dream of smaller, faster, direct-flying airplanes called sonic cruisers (see

Chapter 6, The State of the Art). Millionaire Dennis Tito has gone one stage further in the redefinition of air travel by making space a destination for the fare-paying tourist (see Chapter 6). As fast as one branch of travel pushes into the new millennium in the Olympian search for further, faster, higher, so another kind of tourism grows, looking for a slower and more sedate means of pottering around the planet. Hence the flourishing cruise-ship culture, and even the reappearance of Zeppelins over Germany (currently offering pleasure jaunts over Lake Constance).

Meanwhile, back on earth, travelers with their feet on the ground are becoming increasingly aware that their passage through countries and countryside is achieved at the cost of a huge impact on the environment and on local culture. Historically one of the most fundamental arguments about the definition of travel has been the distinction between the traveler and the tourist. Travelers have always seen themselves as occupying the high ground here: the traveler being a more noble creature, heroic even, while the tourist is a herd animal and the result of a human form of mass production spewed from the maw of a giant industry (one of the world's biggest – see Chapter 5, The Global Dimension). In practice the line between traveler and tourist often seems to come down to the fact that other people are tourists and we ourselves are of course travelers.

One line of thought is that travelers are those who go to foreign lands or locations with a view to enjoying and even immersing themselves in their foreignness. Tourists, on the other hand, are looking for a change of scenery but expect to take their own familiar world with them, complete with its culture and creature comforts. It's an attractive definition, but one that fails to explain business travel. One of the defining hallmarks of business travel as an industry is its apparent dedication to cushioning the traveler not only from his or her surroundings, but also from fellow travelers and certainly, heaven help us, from the tourists. Incidentally, it's a curious fact, but never, and I mean never, do we hear of "business tourism," despite the number of conferences in any industry you care to choose that take place each year in Hawaii, Bangkok, or Bermuda, although companies' headquarters and management are based in Idaho or Ireland.

All of that is changing, however, as concepts such as adventure tourism and ecotourism come to the fore (see Chapter 7, In Practice:

Travel Success Stories and Chapter 8, Key Concepts). Adventure and activity tourism have arisen in response to the growing desire for travel to involve more than sun, sea, sand, and shopping. Today's travelers are scarcely content unless they are given the opportunity to windsurf, hike up hills, submerge themselves in scuba diving, or kayak till they drop. Once travelers visited such spots as Mérida, Venezuela, simply to see the Andes. Now Mérida has been transformed into an adventure base where rock climbing, paragliding, mountain biking, and horse riding have shouldered their way on to the tourist agenda and into the local economy.

The Earth Summits at Rio and Kyoto have monopolized the news agenda. There is growing awareness of the fragility of the globe we trot, and individuals and industry alike are waking up to the need for tourism to be sustainable if we are to continue to enjoy travel in ten or twenty years' time. Ecotourism and ecotravel (the two words are used pretty much synonymously) is perhaps the clearest example of the way in which travel is now as much about self-definition as it is about transportation. In particular, ecotourism asks whether travelers prefer to see themselves as part of the problem or as part of the solution. It shifts the focus away from the idea of tourists taking their own culture with them, and instead seeks to turn them into a means of preserving the culture of somewhere else. True ecotourism entails education of locals and tourists alike, as well as economics that benefit and preserve the location in question. Fervent supporters of ecotourism would argue that it is the best hope we have for maintaining the ecology of threatened ecosystems, of ensuring that flora, fauna, and folk are all still there for future generations.

From the point of view of an observer of travel, it also brings about one of the biggest reversals in the nature of travel since Thomas Cook invented the package tour (see Chapter 3, The Evolution of Travel). Ecotourism educates the tourist. Ecotourism can even engage the tourist in work to survey and maintain the environment (see Coral Cay Conservation in Chapter 7). Ecotourism transforms the tourist into a guardian of the globe. It has finally turned the whole traveler/tourist debate on its head by clearly handing the high moral ground to the tourist – a re-definition truly as fundamental as Mr Tito's brief foray beyond the drag of gravity.

KEY LEARNING POINTS

» Travel is offering previously unreachable destinations to numbers of people never before dreamed of.

» In doing so, it is diversifying to provide choices that go far beyond the simple issues of getting from A to B.

» As such, part of the process of travel is about personal self-definition, every bit as much as it is about transportation.

The Evolution of Travel

» The development of package tours – Thomas Cook
» The advent of powered flight at the beginning of the twentieth century
» The Jet Age
» Airline deregulation
» The development of different classes in flying and the Frequent-Flyer Program
» The Space Age
» A timeline.

Pedants will presumably point out that the history of travel goes back at least as far as the first pedestrian, and therefore the existence of the human leg. Others will choose to take the birth date of transportation as being around 4000 BC in Mesopotamia or Asia with the invention of the wheel, the Sumerian two-wheeled chariot, or the adoption of sail and oars on boats. The steam engine, the Industrial Revolution, the internal combustion engine, the Wright brothers – there are as many starting points in the history of travel as there are means of travel itself.

However, for the purposes of the Express Exec, the story really begins in 1841 with a 32-year-old printer and former Baptist preacher named Thomas Cook. Cook was in the habit of walking from his home in Market Harborough to the nearby town of Leicester to attend temperance meetings. In common with not a few Victorians, he believed that alcohol was at the root of most, if not all, evil. He felt that if an alternative occupation to drinking could be found to consume the working man's time and money then the world would be a better place. Ironically, of course, this was to lead in due course to the serve-yourself business lounge bar, the in-flight drinks trolley, and eventually full-blown bars, booziness, and hangovers 10km up in the air.

Cook was not to know that, however, and at one such meeting he proposed that a train be used to take the teetotalers to a delegate meeting in Loughborough. The Midland Railway Company agreed, and on July 5, 1841, 500 passengers were taken 19km (12 miles) there and back for a shilling. It was the first package holiday.

In 1855 the International Exhibition in Paris gave Cook a chance to broaden his scope, and despite the reluctance of the cross-Channel companies he was able to offer the more daring tourists of the day a grand circular tour via Brussels, Cologne, the Rhine, Heidelberg, Baden-Baden, Strasbourg, and Paris, returning to London via Le Havre or Dieppe. Previously such an outing was only thinkable for the wealthy, and the revolution of offering it to ordinary folk is hard to comprehend today. Robert Runcie, the late Archbishop of Canterbury, once said, "I sometimes think that Thomas Cook should be numbered among the secular saints. He took travel from the privileged and gave it to the people."

In 1864 Thomas's son John joined the business and two years later conducted travelers on the first US tour. By 1869 Thomas Cook was offering Nile tours and trips to Palestine, and by 1872 the opening of the Suez Canal enabled him to organize his first round-the-world tour. Tourism had just gone global, and for the next quarter-century was to be completely dominated by the name of Thomas Cook.

Boats and planes were thus established as the means of tourist travel while Queen Victoria was still on the throne of England, but it was the beginning of the new century that was to usher in the next major step on the way to today's travel. On December 17, 1903, Orville and Wilbur Wright took to the air at Kitty Hawk, North Carolina, in the first-ever powered flight by a heavier-than-air machine. Balloons and gliders had soared in the skies before this, but that single flight, all 37m of it, was to change the face of travel forever.

In 1914 the first scheduled air service took off in Florida, where Glenn Curtiss was offering a seaplane service across Tampa Bay. It worked but wasn't a success, partly because the route was not in sufficient demand, partly because the public had yet to take planes (noisy, unsafe-looking string bags as they were) to their hearts. It took a number of factors to make that happen, including the US government's use of aircraft to deliver mail, the technological developments of the First World War, and the intervention of Henry Ford, whose Ford Trimotor (better known as the Tin Goose) was a turning point. The Tin Goose of 1927 was the first true passenger plane. It carried twelve passengers, had an aisle, and best of all had the first stewardesses to walk up and down it. In the same year Charles Lindbergh flew non-stop from New York to Paris. In the process he became an all-American hero and aviation became the star of the day. It also led directly to the imposition of jet lag and the red-eye overnight flight.

The jet age, and with it the jet set, actually dates back to Frank Whittle's invention in 1930, but it wasn't until 1952 that the first passenger jet, the Comet, took to the skies and flew from London to Johannesburg. In 1958 came the first US passenger jet, the Boeing 707, and by 1969 the familiar bulbous form of the Jumbo was to be seen overhead. Perhaps more important for the traveler was the 1978 Airline Deregulation Act, which changed the airline industry from one of public utilities to a competitive market. Cynics would point out that the airlines have been trying ever since to create enough alliances to turn the clock back to those pre-competition days. Nonetheless, the Air Transport Association of America calculates that fares have declined more than 35% in real terms since deregulation in 1978. It has certainly had an impact on the number of Americans taking to the skies. The Air Transport Association calculates that in 1977, the last year before deregulation, US airlines carried 240 million passengers. By 1999 they were carrying nearly 640 million.

The way those passengers traveled was changing too. Initially, flying was seen as a special event and even economy travelers would dress up in their Sunday best for boarding. By the 1960s, however, the package holiday boom had led to budget travelers filling the planes, and the demarcation of front of plane and back of plane had become clear. You either had money to burn, and got legroom, or you paid an economy fare and were cramped in what soon became known as "cattle class."

During the late 1970s the airlines caught on to the idea that travelers didn't break down into two distinct groups, and that in particular there were increasing numbers of business travelers who wanted to arrive fresh, with their circulation intact, but whose tickets were paid for by companies with no pretensions to first-class travel. Business Class was invented as a halfway house and remained largely unchanged until Richard Branson's Virgin Atlantic airline ushered in a twist on the tier system in 1985 by introducing Upper Class. This provided first-class service at business-class cost. Middle Class (now Premium Economy) was for those paying the full-rate economy fare, and Economy Class was for those flying discounted economy. The thinking behind it was that many business travelers were being told to fly economy rather than business as recession gripped, and yet were still expected to take long-haul flights. Premium Economy offered that halfway house of legroom without the frills of First.

Meanwhile the degree of luxury was skyrocketing. Business-class passengers can now expect sleeper seats, limousines to and from the airport, in-flight massage, personal entertainment systems with a choice of DVDs, lounges in airports, even a full bar in the air – all far more than first-class passengers could have hoped for a decade ago. Like some kind of benign arms race, the pace of change continues unabated – Delta introduced the 2–2–2 seat configuration (look, ma – no middle seat) and now British Airways, refusing to take this competition lying down, has gone a step further with fully horizontal beds on overnight flights.

Nor are in-flight luxuries the only perks of the Express Exec on the move. In May 1981, American Airlines (AA) introduced AAdvantage, the very first frequent-flyer program. From that day forth, flyers have learnt to judge each other by the color of their loyalty cards. They clutch boarding-card stubs the way their grandparents treasured cigarette cards, and only accept transfers to another airline if it has an alliance with their regular frequent-flyer scheme. In the process they have had to get used to the concept of Air Miles schemes, in which a passenger may require many thousands of Air Miles to complete a journey between airports only a few hundred geographical miles apart.

In order to cope with that volume of ticketing, with frequent-flyer calculations, and with information sharing between airlines, computer reservations systems have had to be put in place. In the nineties the biggest single change to the traveler's life was the opening up of those systems to the consumer in the form of booking sites on the Web. Now the role of the travel agent is changing fast, as simply brokering the deal between traveler and travel provider is not enough. Removing agents from those deals has led to a more streamlined service and a drop in prices that benefits the budget market, while the smarter travel agents have moved into niche marketing and personalization of travel packages.

The budget market has also had a huge boost, in Europe at least, from the proliferation of no-frills airlines. These owe their existence to a move by the European Commission back in 1987 which introduced a ten-year reform process that opened up the European Union countries to any airline holding a valid EU Air Operator's Certificate. That ended the fiefdoms of the old national carriers, which had previously ruled the skies over their home nations, and opened up the way for cost-cutting competition. No-frills airlines with no tickets, no seat reservations, and no "free" meals quickly spanned the Continent with cheap travel. Ryanair and easyJet were among the first, having been formed in 1985 (see Chapter 7, In Practice: Travel Success Stories) and seizing on the EC decision to push into the Continent. Their success prompted British Airways and Virgin to launch their own cheap lines, Go and Virgin Express.

The no-frills airlines have proved an enormous success. Ryanair is one of the most profitable airlines in Europe, despite offering one-way international fares from as little as £5. EasyJet has also blazed a trail by pushing towards 100% Internet sales of its tickets (it currently stands at just under 90%).

Indeed, the competition to such lines is unlikely to come from other air carriers, but may instead come from trains, which are entering a second golden age. The Eurostar service (see Chapter 7, In Practice: Travel Success Stories) connecting London to Paris and Brussels has already stolen much of the business travel from the airlines because of its convenience: there is no luggage check, no queue for security, and no travel out of the center of town to an airport. The opening up of the *TGV Méditerranée* connecting Paris to Marseilles in just three hours may well do the same for much of the holiday and business traffic going down to the Mediterranean. Thomas Cook would be delighted to see that trains, the cornerstone of his original popularization of travel, are making a comeback in the space age.

Undoubtedly the greatest talking point of recent travel has been Dennis Tito's jaunt into space (see Chapter 6, The State of the Art) on the International Space Station, making the multimillionaire Californian the first paying tourist in space. Pundits have been predicting space tourism for decades; indeed, science fiction of the forties and fifties had many of us living there by now. The prohibitive cost ($20mn) means that only a select few will be joining the rocket set in the near future, ensuring that there is still at least one field of travel reserved for the affluent.

In the meantime, the tumbling prices, truly global choice of destinations, and proliferation of special-interest and activity-based travel have led the World Travel and Tourism Council (WTTC – see Chapter 5, The Global Dimension) to predict that in less than a decade over 11% of the world's population will be employed directly or indirectly by the travel and tourism industries.

TIMELINE

» **c. 4000 BC**: In Mesopotamia, someone invents the wheel.
» **1841 (July 5)**: Thomas Cook invents the package tour, taking 500 passengers by train on a 38km round trip from Leicester to Loughborough for a shilling.

» **1860**: A Frenchman, Jean Joseph Etienne Lenoir, devises an internal combustion engine.
» **1866**: John Mason Cook personally conducts the first American tour.
» **1874**: Thomas Cook launches the Circular Note, forerunner of the traveler's check.
» **1869**: Cook's tours extend to Egypt and the Bible Lands.
» **1872**: The Suez Canal leads Cook to open an office in Cairo, and enables him to organize his first world tour.
» **1890s**: The first cars make their appearance.
» **1903 (December 17)**: The first powered flight by a heavier-than-air machine succeeds at Kitty Hawk, North Carolina. The inventors of this new flying machine are brothers Orville and Wilbur Wright, two bicycle makers.
» **1914 (January 1)**: The first scheduled air service begins in Florida: Glenn Curtiss launches a seaplane service for crossing Tampa Bay. It is not a great success.
» **1919**: Thos. Cook & Son advertises tickets for the first public trips by plane.
» **1927 (May 20)**: Charles Lindbergh sets out on an historic flight across the Atlantic Ocean from New York to Paris in the *Spirit of St Louis*.
» **1930**: Frank Whittle, a British pilot, designs the first jet engine.
» **1935**: The first air traffic control tower is established at what today is Newark International Airport in New Jersey. The way is now open for holding stacks, congestion, and air controller industrial action.
» **1952**: A 36-seat British-made jet, the Comet, flies from London to Johannesburg, South Africa, at speeds as high as 500 miles per hour.
» **1957 (October 4)**: The USSR launches Sputnik into earth orbit.
» **1961 (April 12)**: Russian Cosmonaut Yuri Gagarin orbits the Earth in *Vostok 1*.
» **1969 (July 20)**: American astronaut Neil Armstrong becomes the first man to set foot on the Moon.
» **1975**: A joint American – Russian venture docks spacecraft together in space.
» **1977**: The first reusable space shuttle, the US craft *Enterprise*, makes its first test flight.
» **1978**: The Airline Deregulation Act opens up the US airline business to competition.

» **1981 (May)**: American Airlines (AA) introduces AAdvantage, the first frequent-flyer program.

» **1983 (January)**: Marriott Hotels joins the frequent-flyer fray with its own program. Marriott soon follows with its Honored Guest Awards program in November 1983.

» **1987**: The European Commission opens up the skies of Europe by ruling that any European airline can compete on any European route. The way is clear for the no-frills budget airlines.

» **2001 (May)**: Dennis Tito becomes the first paying tourist in space.

» **2001 (June)**: The *TGV Méditerranée* starts to run a service from Paris to Marseilles. The high-speed train thus makes it from Northern Europe to the Mediterranean in just three hours, putting pressure on airlines, which struggle to beat the time/value proposition of the train.

» **2001 (August)**: The Zeppelin airship takes to the skies over Lake Constance in Germany, taking with it the first fare-paying airship passengers since disasters such as the Hindenburg ended the trade in the 1930s.

KEY LEARNING POINTS

» From an historical necessity, in which all travel could be described as being "business travel," travel evolved first into a pleasure for the rich and then into an occupation for the masses by the nineteenth century.

» From there it has evolved in every direction imaginable: on the one hand, reaching for the stars in the case of those seeking exclusivity; and on the other, being within the reach of all.

» Curiously, along the way it has also seen the reinvention of older modes of transport, so that airships, 1880s-style passenger ships, and the train are all back in fashion and in some cases providing rivalry for the most modern forms of air transport.

The E-Dimension

» The flexibility of online booking
» The growth of the online travel booking business
» The glitches
» The advent of Orbitz
» Special needs
» Tips for successful Web booking.

ONLINE TRAVEL BOOKING

Wanderlust and the Web were made for each other. It's not just because you can save money on travel – although you can, and by the bucketful at that. It's not just because the choice of options goes beyond the wildest imaginings of even the best travel agent – which it does. It's not even just because in a couple of clicks you can research, order, and pay for your entire trip – which is (occasionally) true. No, the real joy of the e-dimension for the frequent traveler, whether armchair or out-there, is that you have the chance to be choosy. Not just a little bit choosy, but full-on, in-your-face, try-the-patience-of-a-saint picky about every single little element of time, itinerary, price, and place. Before settling on a final lineup you can chop and change plans by revising routes, checking rival airlines, quizzing fares, changing dates, and seeing who caters for lacto-ovo vegetarian dog owners. Like the sound of Antananarivo but flummoxed as to where it is? No problem – the Web allows you to research the place, the geographical location, and prices from all the major airlines. All at three o'clock in the morning. Try that with your local travel agent.

Whereas conventional travel is based around the idea that you know where you want to go and when, the Web gives you the freedom to play with any or all of the variables. On a budget? Why not set your own price at Priceline (www.priceline.co.uk) and see if any of the tour or flight operators is prepared to do the deal on your terms? Not fussed where you go for a week? Try TravelFinder (www.travelfinder.co.uk), which will e-mail you suggestions every day at your desk. Left it too late? Lastminute.com (www.lastminute.com) has a range of hotels, holidays, and destinations for the spontaneous, the time-strapped, or the terminally disorganized.

Little wonder, then, that online travel is taking off and that the online agencies such as Expedia and Travelocity are fast becoming the first port of call for the travel-curious. Rich Barton, CEO of Expedia, recently told *Fast Company* magazine that "Fifty-nine million Americans used the Internet to research travel last year – that's fast approaching the number of people who actually took trips." Barton is backed up by the money that is changing hands online. A Nielsen/Net Ratings survey shows that in March 2001 alone over a billion dollars was spent on online travel – up nearly 60% on the previous year's figure, and that despite a downturn in the US economy.

Nor is this simply a US phenomenon. The NOP Research Group found that almost half-a-million people in the UK bought their vacations online in the month leading up to the Christmas break in 2000. As for future predictions, Forrester Research reports that the online leisure travel market is set to represent some 14% of all leisure travel sales in the UK by 2005. To do that, it will grow from some £592mn now to a healthy £3.7bn by 2005, of which nearly half will come from online flight sales.

None of this should come as too much of a shock. After all, for years the air travel business has been run behind the scenes by a handful of computerized booking services such as Sabre, Amadeus, WorldSpan, and Galileo. When you use a travel agent, either in person or on the phone, all you've been doing is getting them to query the computer system for you. So by switching to the Web all that we're doing is cutting out the keypunching middleman and in the process getting the option to pose as many questions as a chronically indecisive soul could desire. Better yet, unlike those unmissable offers posted in the window of the average travel agent, the great deals that pop up when you search any of the big online agencies are actually available for purchase.

In the process of shedding the middleman, there is also a huge saving up for grabs for the flight operators. UK no-frills carrier easyJet came to the conclusion a few years ago that in order to fill a jet on a short-haul European trip, the cost of mounting the telesales operation amounts to nearly twice the price of the fuel. The cost of booking on the Web is a fraction of that, and so even if they split the difference with the traveler or provide incentives by offering double the Air Miles for Web-booked flights (as United Airlines has done) they still save money, while offering ever more competitive pricing. EasyJet has proved keen to put its money where its mouth is, so much so that it now claims to sell over 80% of its flights online, a figure that is rising. If that trend continues, such cheap flights may well become the exclusive preserve of the Web.

Of course, it hasn't been without its problems. The linking up of back-end booking systems and a consumer front end (the Web) has been less than seamless and tales are legion of consumers going through a lengthy booking procedure only to have the system crash in the middle of the payment process. Logistics have sometimes posed a problem too, since the back-end booking systems have never had to issue tickets, and some of the new online agencies had done little to prepare for demand. Lastminute.com, for example, used to allow users to go through screen after screen of flight selection and payment options before declaring that since they wanted to fly within three days they would now have to complete the transaction by telephone. Given that the whole point of the site was for people aiming to leave at short notice, this was less than ideal. Other sites went the opposite way and played for safety, so that when Expedia launched in the UK, for example, it did not take bookings for the current month, in order to ensure that tickets could be issued in time. All of these irritations are being ironed out, but the process hasn't been entirely painless and can still prove less than perfect.

Despite such glitches, however, the online travel industry has prospered in leaps and bounds. It's a process that has seen the big names such as Expedia (the offspring of Microsoft and now majority-owned by USA Networks), and Travelocity (a subsidiary of the airline booking system company Sabre) burst their way into the ranks of the top travel agents of any kind. The rest of the travel industry could hardly fail to notice, and after watching the leading lights exploit the benefits of Web travel the race is now on to become the world's most popular airline online.

In June 2001 the stakes were raised in this contest by the creation of Orbitz, a bid by five of the biggest US airlines to create the most comprehensive offering on the Net. United, Continental, Delta, Northwest, and American Airlines have come together to create Orbitz (www.orbitz.com), which claims to have established relationships with more than 40 other air carriers, hotels, and car rental companies so as to give consumers a greater choice than ever. US consumers have promptly responded by lobbying the government to block the site's launch until Orbitz assures regulators that it will operate on a level playing field. To date Orbitz has been given the green light by antitrust regulators, but the US consumers' concern is well founded, given that airlines are busy forming ever broader alliances that threaten to reduce cost-cutting competition between them.

Orbitz is clearly unlikely to usher in any competition between the five founder airlines, but what it may well do is to up the ante with the likes of Expedia and Travelocity by introducing a Web price war. The time certainly appears to be right – warnings of economic slowdown are leading to tightening travel budgets, yet at the same time the online travel sector is showing healthy growth. Unlike many of the nascent dot.com industries, travel is showing signs of making money hand over fist, leading to the likes of Expedia showing profit nearly a year ahead of predictions. If there's an area that can afford a bit of competitive head-to-head, this is it; and the signs are that Orbitz is only the beginning.

On the other side of the Atlantic the European airlines have clearly seen the writing on the wall and responded in turn with their own online alliance. Opodo (the name comes from "opportunity to do") is the brainchild of Aer Lingus, Air France, Alitalia, Austrian Airlines, British Airways, Finnair, Iberia, KLM, and Lufthansa, who have all come together to create their own online travel service specializing in cheap flights and holidays. Former Alitalia CEO, Giovanni Bisignani, the man set to take the reins at the new venture, told the BBC that "Europe has for some time lagged behind the US for online travel bookings and we believe that Europe is about to witness an explosion in demand for online travel services surpassing US growth by as early as 2004." In order to do that, Opodo says it will be offering discounted flights from nearly 500 airlines, as well as offers on accommodations from over 54,000 hotels. The plan is to launch in the major European countries over the next couple of years and from there to the nations of each of the founder airlines.

It remains to be seen what effect Orbitz and Opodo will have on pricing. Cutthroat competition can only be good news for consumers, although these large alliances are a source for concern – airlines aren't in the business of teaming up with rivals in order to reduce travelers' expenditure. Price is not, however, the only factor in travel, and in addition to the bulk deals and cheap costs of online travel there is also an increasing move towards niche marketing and the personalization of trips.

As well as hooking up to the central booking computers directly – what you might see as a vertical connection – the Web allows for some pretty lateral connections that link up a lot of small companies, in the process providing ever greater consumer choice. In the business, this leads into what's known as "complex travel," which is a relative term.

For an industry that's used to carving the whole of humanity into three groups – first, business, and cattle – the complexity is about taking into account individual choices and needs. That could mean those who need to travel with their pets or those looking for a religious pilgrimage. At its extreme it could be very niche-market, such as non-smoking vegetarian whale watchers with the need for wheelchair access on board, but as often as not it's more common sense than complex. Many tour operators offer cruise-ship holidays, for example, and it's well established that these are popular with senior members of society. But how many can assure you that wheelchair access is available not only throughout the ship, but also on shore at ports of call?

Taking care of specific needs is something the Web does well because it can poll a vast number of disparate sources rapidly. Some companies, such as eGulliver.com (www.egulliver.com) have come to specialize in putting together holidays for those with special needs (ghost spotting, anyone?), and so the future of Web travel is not simply as a vast discount travel agency controlled by the airlines. Indeed, as price competition becomes tougher we are likely to see ever more inventive ways of differentiation as sites struggle to be different. Lastminute.com, for example, has just added an "adult" section to its travel site – amorous adventurers can order paint-on chocolate or edible underwear to accompany them on their travels, or for around £10 you can buy an inflatable wife or husband to provide silent moral support on that grueling business trip. Of course, you might have a job explaining that one away if you're stopped at Customs, but at least you can always tell them that, thanks to the Web, it's merely a taste of things to come in travel.

Best practice: tips for browsing and booking travel online

There's no doubt about it, when it's all going well then buying online is the quickest, most efficient way of booking travel short of having a telepathic travel agent at your disposal. That's in an ideal world. Back in the real world, however, there are catches and there are ways around them.

Firstly, shop around. Expedia may have come up with the goods for your friends and colleagues, but it doesn't mean that it's the only one for you. In part this is because different airlines do deals with different sites, so that, for example, Southwest Airlines are not to be found on Expedia or Travelocity (apparently because of computer compatibility). KLM recently decided to eliminate commissions paid to booking sites, which means that it is suddenly less popular than other airlines and where present may incur a surcharge.

Perhaps most important of all for budget travelers, most of the no-frills flyers such as easyJet do not sell through travel agents of any kind, Web sites included, and so the only way to check their fares (often the cheapest available) is to go direct to their sites. The smart advice therefore is not only to poll the likes of Travelocity, Expedia, and Lastminute.com, but also to go direct to the sites of the no-frills to see if their destination map tallies with your travel itinerary (addresses for all of these are in Chapter 9, Resources). For some routes British users may still find it cheaper to pick up the phone – much of the airline inventory on offer comes from US carriers, transatlantic flights, and continental Europe. For routes out to the Indian subcontinent and Africa, these are often beaten by the traditional discount travel agencies that have long specialized in those routes.

Beware of small print, too. When you're booking online, there's no travel agent to explain the limitations of tickets or deals. Nine times out of ten this will not be a problem but you can bet your bottom dollar that the one time you have to change your plans you will find that special restrictions apply to tickets bought online for the airline you're traveling with. The information is almost always available at the point of sale (in this case on your computer screen), but there are some interesting interpretations of "available" that can mean digging through the small print.

Compare pricing carefully – "discount" famously does not mean the lowest price, and some cheaper flights manage to cut that cost by flying to airports that are not usually considered to be the obvious choice for your city destination. It's very easy if you don't know your way around a foreign city to accept that "such and such" is the name of the nearest airport only to find that it isn't and that the taxi ride will cost you the best part of your saving on the discount ticket.

Used properly, the Web is a fabulous research tool, but it is firmly attached to the cynical commercial world we all inhabit, so never presume that search engines are unbiased or exhaustive. Many online booking engines allow you to hold a booking for a period of 12 or 24 hours before you have to make your mind up and show your money – feel free to use that facility to reserve a deal while looking for something better. Be aware, however, that all this does is hold the seat, not the fare, so there's no guarantee you'll get that same great deal when you go back the next day.

Don't forget that the air fare is just a part of your travel expenses and that discounts on accommodations, taxis, auto rental, and even theme parks, meals, and show tickets are all available. Finally, as a wild card, when you've finished researching prices and availability on your chosen itinerary, why not go to Priceline and put in an offer undercutting anything you've seen so far? It just might work.

KEY LEARNING POINTS

» Online sites offer unrivaled opportunities for researching destinations and itineraries.

» Online booking sites cut out the middleman (usually the travel agent) and leave you free to experiment ad infinitum, juggling schedules and alternative dates and destinations.

» Online booking sites are rarely completely unbiased, since they often rely on reservation engines that cater for a reduced range of airlines.

» Not all the best deals online come from travel agents – some are direct from suppliers' sites.

» Such are the savings for the tour and travel operators that some tickets and tours will soon be available exclusively online.

The Global Dimension

- » Transcontinental holiday competition
- » Size of the industry
- » Predictions of growth
- » The world leaders
- » The destinations of tomorrow
- » Best practice – protecting yourself in a big world, and protecting the world from a big industry.

Few businesses can be more global than travel. Cheaper flights, ever-expanding routes, fast-breeding hotel chains and a vogue for adventure travel mean that this little blue-green planet is now crisscrossed daily by backpackers and business travelers alike.

It wasn't always that way. Right up until the 1960s, international travel beyond immediate neighbor countries remained the preserve of an elite group of privileged people blessed either with deep pockets or with a lot of time on their hands. Now, however, the world has opened up to mass tourism, and the increasing globalization of industries mean that many of us work for companies with offices in other counties, countries, or continents. In the process the choices open to the traveler have exploded, and the travel business has found itself opening the paths for competition where previously it would have been unthinkable. In the early 1990s when EuroDisney opened at Marne la Vallée outside Paris, it quickly had to come to terms with the fact that its biggest competition for British visitors did not come from any of the other theme parks in Europe. A strong franc and the competition among transatlantic carriers meant that it was cheaper for a typical family to take their vacation at Disneyland in Orlando rather than cross the Channel. Florida, rather than France, was to become the first family vacation abroad for many children of a new generation. We are all now traveling further, faster, and for less money.

In the process, travel is turning into a global business in terms not only of its reach, but also of the amount of money it represents. Travel and tourism don't only impact on travel companies and resorts; they also account for spending on support services, infrastructure, food, drink, and raw materials. According to some sources, tourism is now the world's fastest growing industry, and according to the World Travel and Tourism Council (WTTC) it is the world's largest generator of wealth and jobs. Travel and tourism are fast coming to represent a sizeable share of the Gross Domestic Product (GDP) for industrialized and underdeveloped nations alike. In fact tourism is now reckoned to be the world's number one export earner, ahead of automotive products, chemicals, petroleum, and food.

The WTTC, a global forum for evaluating the full economic impact of travel and tourism, predicts that by 2011 the travel and tourism economy will constitute 11% of global GDP. As part of this, it will directly or indirectly support 260,417,000 jobs worldwide, which in turn represent 9% of total employment or 1 in 11.2 jobs on the planet. Nor will it stop there. According to the Madrid-based World Tourism Organization (WTO), the number of international tourists is set to rise even further to some 1.55 billion by the year 2020.

The year 2000 proved to be something of a turning point for the travel and tourism business. Aside from the millennium-inspired globetrotting, there were also a number of international attractions dotted around the globe, including the Olympic Games in Sydney, the Euro 2000 European football championship, Expo 2000, and the Vatican Jubilee. These all conspired to push up international tourist arrivals by 7.4% – the highest growth rate in a decade. Some 700 million people ventured abroad in 2000, spending an estimated $476bn in the process, which, according to a study carried out by the University of Lausanne for the WTO, led to tourism representing somewhere between 4% and 6% of the GDP of industrialized countries. Not bad for a single industry.

Let's look at some examples from the WTO study. Australia generates A$58.2bn from domestic and international tourism combined, representing 4.5% of GDP and accounting for 388,500 jobs – 5.4% of the total Australian workforce. New Zealand generates NZ$9.1bn from domestic and international tourism combined, representing 3.4% of GDP. Tourism accounts for 58,000 jobs, which may not sound like much until you realize that for the sparsely populated Land of the Long White Cloud it represents over 4% of the workforce. Canada, a seemingly less touristy destination, nonetheless generates C$54.1bn from domestic and international tourism, which adds up to 2.4% of the Canadian GDP. That in turn translates to 546,400 jobs, about 3.5% of the national workforce.

Perhaps the biggest surprise is France. Tourism there accounts for 624,400 jobs or only 2.7% of the French workforce, and yet the amount of money involved, some F.Fr.605bn, means that tourism accounts for a full 7.3% of the country's GDP. Back in 1998 France was singled out as the world's number one destination, and also benefits from the fact that a great many French people choose to take their vacations in different parts of their own country. All in all it means that *l'exception Française* has proved to be a nice little earner despite the fact that relatively few French workers seem to be involved.

Right now the world's most visited country is the US, although the WTO predicts that by 2020 it will lose that crown to another big country – China. Despite the problems of the Asian financial crisis in the late nineties, East Asia and the Pacific region is the area where travel is expanding the fastest. Of course, for long-haul travelers the financial crisis only served to make the area more attractive by weakening local currencies and making regional travel cheaper. At the International Tourism Fair of 1998 it was reported that destinations in East Asia and the Pacific were suffering. International tourist arrivals had declined by 1.2%, and more importantly earnings were down by 4%. Countries that depended on Asian tourists, notably Australia, New Zealand, Indonesia, the Philippines, Hong Kong, and Singapore were the worst hit. Even so, the resilience of both the region and the industry allowed Francesco Frangialli, WTO Secretary General, to predict that "judging from middle and long-term forecasts, which have been revised in the light of the Asian and Russian crises, we can bank on a return to sustained growth within the next two years – provided we are not faced with any new large-scale upheavals."

Frangialli has been proved right, and a general resurgence in the area sees the WTO tipping East Asia to overtake North America (including Mexico, Canada, and the US), pushing the continent out of second place and into third by the year 2020. Europe looks set to remain the continent most visited overall.

Which is not to say that it's all doom and gloom for the US travel market. If anything the change is partly because Americans are looking beyond their own national boundaries in increasing numbers. Despite the international jokes about George W. Bush's lack of worldwide travel prior to his Presidency, in that respect at least he is a pretty fair representative of his people. As recently as 1995 the vast majority of travel from the North American continent went no further than Canada or Mexico. Indeed, intra-regional travel within the continent accounted for 77% of all tourist arrivals. According to the latest WTO report – *Tourism 2020 Vision; Americas* – that's about to change, dropping to 62% as the proportion of long-haul travelers leaving the continent rises from 27% to 31%. In other words, watch out, world – the Americans are coming.

Well, watch out Europe, actually, since it is expected to retain its ranking as the number one long-haul destination region. Indeed, its numbers are expected to rise by nearly 3% a year, which, curiously, is about the same figure by which the proportion of outbound Americans is expected to rise.

Outside Europe, the Caribbean is fully expected to continue to draw US tourists, although the biggest single change there depends on whether, as is widely predicted, the US lifts travel restrictions for Americans going to Cuba. Ever since Fidel Castro nationalized American-owned companies during the Cold War, US citizens have been faced with fines if they break the embargo on travel to the Caribbean island. That hasn't stopped Cuba becoming one of the top tourist destinations of the region, however, and other island resorts are dreading the day that the communist resort is finally declared within bounds for US tourists. On the presumption that this day is near, the WTO predicts that Cuba will see an average rise in the number of tourists of 9.2% a year to 6.7 million, with the US alone expected to account for 2.3 million of Cuba's tourists by 2020.

Meanwhile, the bulk of those travelers bound Stateside will continue to come from the "old countries" of Europe. There are some changes in the offing, though, not least a surge in the number of Japanese visitors, who are predicted to increase annually by over 7%. That means that Japanese visitors will outnumber those from Mexico or Canada. Indeed, if true it would mean that about one in four of predicted international tourists in the US will be from the Land of the Rising Sun.

Aside from those travelers going either to or from the US, the regions that are growing the fastest as destinations are Africa and the Middle East. Of all the regions in the world, the one showing the fastest growth, inshallah, is the Middle East, which is expected to see visitor numbers grow annually by 7.5% as more and more tourists warm to its charms. It has to be said, though, that this figure was arrived at before the current escalation of violence in the Israeli/Palestinian conflict. In the light of the suicide bombings and the helicopter missile attacks in Palestinian territories, those figures are doubtless being revised downwards as attractions such as Eilat and Jerusalem lose some of their appeal.

Africa, too, is a region with huge travel potential but blighted by fears for the security of tourists. That problem is further heightened by infrastructure problems, conflict between nations, and in some cases a degree of suspicion clouding relations between the public and private sectors. That said, the WTO envisages tourist arrivals in Africa reaching 77.3 million in 2020, up from 27.8 million in 2000 – a tripling of numbers. Of those the biggest change is a move away from the Northern African countries of the Maghreb, which in light of disturbances in Algeria really means the tourist trails of Morocco and Tunisia. These have benefited from Mediterranean beaches and, in the case of Morocco, inclusion in European-wide train-ticket schemes. As such they are likely to maintain their appeal, but not as much as the growth areas of southern and eastern Africa. Southern Africa, which includes Namibia, Zambia, Lesotho, and Swaziland as well as South Africa, is forecast to enjoy an average 10.4% annual rise in arrivals, up from 7.9 million in 2000 to over 36 million by 2020, overtaking the North African region in the process. By contrast, Tunisia and Morocco will see much slower growth: Tunisia by 3% a year, from 5 million in 2000 to 9 million by 2020; and Morocco with 5% annual growth, from 4 million in 2000 to 8.7 million by 2020. East Africa is expected to grow up to 6% annually, a rise aided by the increasingly professional management of the natural attractions of Uganda, Kenya, and Tanzania, as well as a decline in threat factor from troubles in Rwanda and Burundi.

South Africa is expected to become the biggest source of outbound African travelers, representing nearly half of all outbound Africans by 2020 and dominating inter-regional travel in the area. Of non-African travelers to the continent, Europeans will still provide the majority of travelers. There will be changes, though, as the usual supply of visitors from ex-colonial countries are likely to find themselves traveling alongside a new wave of tourists from eastern Europe as well as East Asia and the Pacific as the region recovers from its economic downturn.

There is no region of the world where travel and tourism are predicted to decline. The industry of travel looks set to continue its explosive growth, and we are not predicted to be getting any the less footloose. According to the WTTC, in less than a decade over 11% of the population will be employed directly or indirectly by tourism. Which means that more than one in ten of us will be working to keep the wheels of travel in motion – when we're not taking time off to travel ourselves, that is.

BEST PRACTICE: GLOBAL TRAVEL, TAKING CARE OF YOURSELF AND YOUR GLOBE

As we all travel further afield and even the more self-contained nations begin to explore beyond their borders, we will inevitably find ourselves in environments and situations that are unfamiliar to us. That is often the principal reason for going there in the first place. It is possible now for an inexperienced traveler simply to buy a ticket, board a plane and go to a neck of the global woods that was once reserved only for the hardy and courageous adventurers of legend. This increases the onus on today's global travelers to take care of both the things at risk: firstly themselves, and secondly the place they find themselves in.

Taking care of yourself starts before the tickets are even bought. Most governments have Foreign Offices/Departments that issue guidelines on safe places to visit and sensible precautions to take in the less safe ones. The standard advice on the less reassuring destinations is just to check in with your local consulate or embassy on arrival and departure – it may sound mothering, but it's good advice. When traipsing down the road less traveled, the more people who know where you're going, the greater your chance of getting there in one piece. For the UK there is advice and a list of consulates and embassies on the Foreign Office Website (www.fco.gov.uk); for the US there is the State Department travel section (www.state.gov/travel.cfm).

Good guidebooks and Websites will help give you a feel for risks and hurdles to overcome, and word-of-mouth advice (often available on Web bulletin boards) is a great step towards being suitably streetwise when you arrive. You might also want to take a look at the Control Risks Group security advice for business travelers (www.crg.com). Medical advice on hazards and preventative medicine should be taken in good time before departure so that there is plenty of time to take courses of injections, etc. Many of the travel sites provide advice for travelers, as does the US Center for Disease Control (www.cdc.gov/travel/bluesheet.htm). Don't forget that inevitably the most useful part of any medical kit is full insurance cover.

Having taken steps to protect yourself on global wanderings, it's then time to spare a thought for the globe itself. It's a lucky traveler who returns to an old haunt and finds it improved; most of us tend to grumble about tourists having ruined the place. The difficulty is how to be part of the solution, not the problem. As with any industry in a period of rampant growth there are concerns about the sustainability of travel and tourism – all the more so since it is the state of the planet itself that is at stake, and very visibly so. The impact of travel and tourism on heavily urbanized areas is one thing – it's unlikely that Manhattan dwellers are going to notice the impact of the predicted Japanese influx over the next ten to fifteen years. The growing trend towards travel further and further off the beaten track, however, gives cause for more immediate concern. Ever since the Rio Earth Summit there has been growing awareness of the part travel and tourism have to play in the future of the environment, and the year 2002 has been designated as the International Year of Ecotourism. When in doubt, don't forget the old motto of travel to the far-flung: "Take nothing but pictures, leave nothing but footprints."

KEY LEARNING POINTS

> Travel has simply never been more global in scope.
> It is the world's largest employer and the fastest growing industry.
> The US is currently the world's most visited country, but may well soon be superseded by China, and Japanese tourists will soon outnumber Canadian and Mexican visitors to the States.
> Meantime, US travelers are ever more likely to leave the US in their travels, the transatlantic routes to Europe looking set to continue to be the world's busiest.

The State of the Art

» Space travel
» Corporate aviation and private jets
» Ticketless travel and biometric identification
» Super-Jumbos and sonic cruisers
» Net surfing in the sky.

SPACE TRAVEL

Space tourism was once the preserve of science fiction and of the many futurists who told us that by the year 2000 we'd all be wearing shiny jumpsuits and commuting to work in our private autogyros. It took Californian multimillionaire Dennis Tito, an increasingly cash-strapped Russian space industry, and some $20mn to turn the fantasy of space tourism into reality, but in May 2001 the dream became fact.

As with so many travel plans, there were a few glitches: delays, computer errors, that kind of thing, plus one or two issues that don't generally bother the more conventional traveler. For a start, Tito was originally scheduled to stay in the Mir space station. A company, Mircorp, had even been formed to exploit Mir's potential as a combined laboratory, film set, and orbital hotel. Unfortunately, Mir, a little creaky after 15 successful years in space, was finally deemed to have passed its sell-by date. It was brought down from orbit, expiring in a blaze of glory and metal fatigue, which rather messed up that particular tourism idea.

Ever a resourceful body, however, the Russian space agency immediately seized on the possibility of using the new International Space Station (ISS). True, the Russians were only one of five partner countries responsible for the new station, but Tito had already paid his money and started his training with the cosmonauts at Moscow's Star City. Besides, the crew commander on the ISS at the time happened to be a Russian. Tito's tour was back on.

NASA was not very pleased, claiming safety concerns. Leading figures such as former astronaut John Glenn came forward to protest. Glenn told CNN, "I don't blame him wanting to go up, and he's right. It's an incredible experience ... But I just think it's a misuse of the spacecraft, and it was supposed to be for research." This was a little ironic, since Glenn himself, by now a US Senator, was taken up as a passenger in the Space Shuttle, the key difference being that he didn't have to pay out of his own pocket.

However, the Russians shrugged off such protests, promising to pay any damage, and rather curiously accusing the US of having already flouted safety by installing an overweight running machine on the station. Certainly the spacemen didn't seem to object. Britain's *Guardian* newspaper reported one of the astronauts on board, James Voss, as saying "We will welcome anybody who shows up at our hatch." Well, you'd like to think they wouldn't turn anyone away at that point.

In the end the Russians prevailed, and 60-year-old Tito got to realize a dream he had first had when an engineer at NASA some 40 years previously. Blasting off in a Soyuz rocket with two fellow astronauts, he successfully reached the Space Station and had an uneventful time, seemingly spent largely in looking out the window, albeit with a view afforded by no other hotel on or off Earth. Returning again via Soyuz, he came to earth with a bump as the recovery capsule touched down near Arkalyk, some 250 miles west of Astana, the capital of Kazakhstan. CNN reported Tito as saying that it had all been "10 times better" than expected; "It was perfect. It was paradise."

It was not so perfect that he was planning to return, however. Tito's comment on the trip was that, far from doing it again, he wanted "other people to make it instead" – which is where it all gets interesting.

Tito used a press interview at Star City to stress that he is keen to act as a middleman between the various space agencies and Wall Street in order to help facilitate space tourism in the future. Russia has clearly stated that it sees tourism as a way of funding further research. Yury Koptev, head of Russia's space agency, told the partners of the ISS that there are a lot more people who want to go, and that money from space visitors would be crucial for the Russian program, although future jaunts aren't envisaged until the Space Station is completed in 2006. Moscow newspapers have speculated that ten would-be spacemen are already in talks with the agency, and film maker James Cameron has reportedly expressed keen interest, presumably in search of an unforgettable camera angle. Tereza Predescu of Space Adventures (the agency responsible for Tito's trip) explained, "Space Adventures is working to put more space tourists like Mr Tito into space; in fact, the next space tourist might be Mr Mark Shuttleworth, a South African millionaire. Despite the $20mn price, we have quite a few people interested in future orbital flights to the ISS."

For the moment it is mainly the Russians who are making the running on this idea. Despite the news that Buzz Aldrin, second man on the moon, has welcomed the idea of using unused Space Shuttle seats to raise money, the US government seems less keen. NASA chief Daniel Goldin has implied that Mr Tito is not a patriot, as he defied the US space agency in order to fulfill his dream. Announcements from the US government seem to be focused more on militarizing space than on opening it up for amateur space travelers.

Nonetheless, some of the technologies being explored by the military have obvious applications for civilian travel. One of the most interesting developments is the scramjet. This is a supersonic development of the ramjet, the idea being that the engine breathes air, so eliminating the need for heavy and expensive liquid oxygen. In theory, scramjet aircraft can reach speeds of Mach 10 (ten times the speed of sound), compared with the Mach 1 or 2 of conventional jets. Tests are still being conducted, though not without hiccups, as the American X-43A aircraft had to be aborted and an Australian effort has currently been delayed; but if tests are successful, one of the abilities of such a craft would be to blast through the atmosphere into near space for short flights, before gliding back down.

The idea is that, instead of taking tourists up to a space station, with the risk that they will interfere with the research there, flights would lift off from the Earth and take a short journey through space, perhaps briefly orbiting the planet before sailing back down to land conventionally like a Space Shuttle. Even if the craft escaped the atmosphere for only a minute or two, it seems that there are plenty of takers who would want to experience the thrust, the weightlessness, and the views. Space Adventures is already looking into taking bookings on travel options that may not even exist yet (more details from www.spaceadventures.com). "SA is currently working with and has exclusive contracts with some of the best private vehicle developers in the space industry," notes Space Adventures' Tereza Predescu, "and is hoping to send people on sub-orbital flights as soon as 2005." The cost of a sub-orbital flight on one of the reusable launch vehicles (RLVs) being developed as part of the X PRIZE is $98,000, and already over 100 people have reserved a place. The RLVs under development for Space Adventures' sub-orbital flights will lead the way towards an entirely new generation of cheaper, more reliable and fully reusable spacecraft. The rocket-powered RLVs will be for two to four passengers.

Certainly space travel is set to remain prohibitively expensive and the preserve of the few. It will be a long time before it joins a week in Marbella or Martha's Vineyard as a holiday option. Even when prices fall, as they inevitably will, it will be a long time before economy of scale becomes an issue.

For some there will still be questions about why on earth you might want to do it anyway. After all, the take-off is likely to terrify all but the staunchest traveler, food and accommodation are sure to be minimal, and frequent-flyer rewards are non-existent. Nausea is common – a Japanese journalist dispatched to Mir reported on little else during his stay – and the physical risks go beyond cramped legroom. If tourists ever manage to stay in space for longer than a brief bout of weightlessness in orbit, they can look forward to muscular atrophy and brittle bones as the calcium drains from them. Yet for all that, space travel remains something of the ultimate travel goal, and possibly irresistible for anyone brought up on spacemen, be they Buck Rogers or Buzz Lightyear. Space tourism, if not yet taking one's vacation in an orbiting hotel, is firmly on the individual travel agenda from here on.

CORPORATE JETS

The executive jet has always been the epitome of corporate glamour. Be it the smallest Lear Jet or a plane with the jumbo proportions of Air Force One, a private jet speaks volumes about power and privilege. There is nothing that confirms the success of the Express Exec more succinctly than a casual reference to "my" jet. For most of us, however, travel in the company jet remains as remote and unlikely as space tourism, particularly if we're not based in the US. While any CEO is going to have to argue hard to convince the accountants and shareholders that they must, just must have a gleaming Gulfstream V parked in the hangar, those outside the States have a doubly high hurdle to clear. About 75% of the world's business jets are to be found in the US; while Europe comes second, it does so with only about a tenth of the world's fleet. That imbalance is down to a number of factors, including air regulations, the size of the single US airspace, and the administration of take-off slots at airports. For all the practicalities and technicalities, however, probably the biggest single reason why US high-flyers do their flying in corporate jets while their European counterparts do it in Club Class is corporate culture.

In Europe, a corporate jet is still regarded very much as a mark of status rather than as sound economics. Selling the idea to shareholders is a tough pitch indeed, not least since the sharper minds won't forget that high-tech private fleets have an uncanny ability to transform into public relations disasters. When Philips went from being the darling of the European high-tech markets to "ailing Dutch electronics giant" in the early nineties, it seemed there wasn't a single newspaper report that missed the fact that the company had the largest private fleet of corporate aircraft on the continent. A generation's hopes of private mile-high travel bought the farm.

The good news for those with airborne ambitions is that corporate aviation is going through a golden era on both sides of the Atlantic. In particular, the signs are that Europe is opening up to the petite yet prestigious world of the company jet.

There are several reasons for this. The advent of cheap, no-frills airlines such as Ryanair, Go, and easyJet has helped challenge the dominance of monopoly national carriers and with them the control of the slot system that limits take-off and landing options. In the US this slot system was abandoned years ago and airports remain open night and day to corporate planes, one of the reasons for the US success story. Better yet, the frustration with the European giants and the limitations of major European hub airports mean that the cheap carriers have breathed new life into smaller regional airports around the continent. Many more airports are being upgraded to take more and more jet traffic, just as restrictions on take-off and landing are eased. At the same time, Europe is introducing a new system of air control that will halve the vertical distance required between planes in the sky, which should help clear the congestion experienced on some routes. Naturally there are environmental and local issues to be taken into account, but the big picture is looking brighter for smaller planes.

While these factors help with the infrastructure, the biggest single boost for corporate aviation comes with a different approach to ownership, one that can probably be ascribed to one company and one man's vision.

Warren Buffet, *entrepreneur extraordinaire*, is the man behind NetJets, the largest fractional-ownership air company in the world. The idea is simple enough. Private jets are prohibitively expensive to buy, to run, and to staff. This meant they were the preserve of the mega-rich, the absurdly profligate, or those with enough friends to get together and share the outlay. Sharing in consortia was a well-established way of cutting the cost and getting the most out of an aircraft, but had its own problems in terms of who administered it and who got to use it when. Fractional ownership comes into play when you ask what happens if you combine the cost benefits of a consortium purchase with the convenience of a management company that sorts out the administration, minimizes costs, and takes care of the logistical headaches of multiple ownership. Fractional-ownership pioneer NetJets has been in operation only since 1998, yet fractional ownership now looks set to dominate corporate aviation.

Under this scheme your company buys into a part-share of a jet, normally a sixteenth, in return for which you get so many hours (normally around forty) of flying time per year. The advantage over a consortium is that the fractional-ownership company doesn't have just one plane; NetJets will soon have a fleet of more than 50 in Europe. So you are unlikely to find that your shared plane is in Stockholm just when you want to take off from Sicily – indeed, you can normally insist on your flying demands being satisfied if you give six hours' notice.

Once you've taken away the pain of buying a plane outright, have ensured that you have access when you need it, and are not paying for it when you don't need it, the cost of corporate aviation starts to become more reasonable. In its special report on corporate aviation, *EuroBusiness* magazine compared a busy round trip in Europe taking in Cardiff, Prague, Milan, Toulouse, and Brussels (among others). It compared the cost of a private jet and a scheduled airline itinerary and found that the scheduled airlines, partly because of the hotel costs enforced by flight times and ticket restrictions, not only took three times as long but actually cost nearly half as much again. That was without adding in the value of the executive's time saved by the company.

Charter companies, the alternative to fractional ownership for the more ad hoc user, work on the basis that with high-earning executives the time-saving on private jets will almost certainly recoup the outlay. The fact that private jets can land at some 450 or so more airports in Europe than are serviced by charter flights only increases the chances of major time-savings. The final proof positive that corporate aviation can please the accountants as well as the flyers is that Richard Branson's Virgin organization is said to be considering a fractional-ownership division. So smart execs. who do their homework and play their cards right may yet find themselves being compelled to take private jets on the strict orders of the more penny-pinching shareholders.

TICKETLESS TRAVEL AND BIOMETRICS

Imagine walking up to a machine, looking into an eyepiece and being immediately able to board the plane with your seat and diet preferences instantly confirmed, your identity established (thereby doing away with passport checks), and your frequent-flyer miles logged on the spot. That's one of the tantalizing promises being waved in front of travelers by a combination of biometric identification and ticketless travel, and it's just one of a number of schemes being tried out right now in airports around the globe.

Ticketless travel means different things depending on which side of the Atlantic you start your journey. In Europe it remains rare; most European travelers still expect to find themselves clutching a precious fistful of red carbon papers, complete with a full copy of the Warsaw Convention on baggage printed on the back. Losing these scraps of paper incurs a price penalty that varies from airline to airline but can amount to the original full price of the ticket. This is despite the fact that the ticket holder can produce identification and establish the right to travel – the only new cost incurred is in printing the red carbon paper. The full ridiculousness of paper tickets becomes clear if ever, like the author, you find yourself at a hub airport, looking to buy a connecting flight, only to find that in order to get the flight you want you have to call a travel agent in the nearest city, so that they can issue and courier the ticket to you at the airport, where they will find you standing by the head ticketing office of the airline you are about to fly with.

In the States most flights are or can now be ticketless. In Europe the new generation of no-frills flyers have been among the first to do away with tickets. If you book with easyJet or Go, your confirmation comes in the form of a fax or e-mail. You just turn up, show a passport, and that's it – in the case of easyJet there aren't even boarding cards as such, since no seats are assigned and the plane just fills up in one smooth flow of boarders from front to back.

That's great for the no-frills, but the problems of ticketless travel have been noted in the US whenever there is a need for a change of plan. In particular, disruption from strikes by airline personnel has caused huge problems as travelers try to switch to different carriers (with different and unconnected computer systems) but with no proof of their travel status. Since nobody but the courier companies could want a return to tickets, the answer has to be some kind of portable information carrier that positively identifies the traveler, but that can store amendments to itineraries.

In Europe, home of the smart card (basically a credit card with a memory chip on it), Lufthansa and Air France have both been experimenting with smart cards for frequent flyers. The Air France smart card and Lufthansa ChipCard both use radio technology, so that the holder needs only to walk past a reader at the gate for the card and its details to be read. If inserted into a standard card reader, the Lufthansa ChipCard goes a step further: it can be used as a German telephone card, a credit card, a frequent-flyer miles card, and an ID for business lounges at European airports.

The smart card, however, is only one of several technologies being looked into. Another avenue of approach is to do away with cards or devices and use the individual body itself as means of confirming details. The US company EyeTicket has a system of iris recognition that uses a simple video camera to examine the colored ring around the pupil of the eye. Irises are as individual as fingerprints, and checking the iris with a camera is a great deal less intrusive than, say, beaming a laser into your eyeball as is required for the retinal scanning you may have seen in spy movies. Having recognized the iris in question from a database of frequent-flyers' iris images, the system then comes back with the appropriate passport number, frequent-flyer ID, and travel details, in theory taking care of everything from check-in to baggage check, boarding, and passport control.

Right now the system is in use at London Heathrow in a trial involving several thousand North American citizens using Virgin Atlantic and British Airways. All are frequent visitors to the UK and all have previously been cleared by passport control. The EyeTicket system checks their identities and allows them to pass without having to dig out their passports. If you've ever seen the "non-European citizen" queues at points of entry to the UK, you'll understand what a major leap forward that represents for the time-strapped traveler.

The trial is being conducted in conjunction with IATA, and should it prove successful it will perhaps pave the way for further biometric applications such as check-in and the processing of frequent-flyer miles. There may be an end in sight to all those hours spent stuck in queues, with nothing but the Warsaw Convention and our passport stamps for entertainment.

SUPER-JUMBOS, SONIC CRUISERS, AND SURFING IN THE SKY

The shape of things to come is already being decided by the airplane makers and would appear to come in a number of different forms. Boeing, the dominant manufacturer of outsize passenger jets since the advent of the Jumbo 747 in the late 1960s, has been displaced by a European consortium with its vision of the new generation of super-jumbos. The Airbus A380 super-jumbo has by now received more than enough orders to enable final production to go ahead. It is intended to fly up to 800 people into hub airports, and has so much space in its double-decked airframe that some airlines may incorporate beds and a gymnasium into their luxury-class cabins. Boeing had been exploring the same route with a project dubbed the "hotel in the sky"; but having seen the Airbus snap up the orders, it has since switched to an entirely different approach to air travel, one that allows faster flying for a smaller number of passengers from point to point, avoiding hubs and stopovers.

The new project, dubbed the Sonic Cruiser, is as yet little more than a collection of models, sketched plans, and what-if scenarios that won't be finalized until the Seattle-based airplane maker has finished discussions with its potential client airlines. The basic idea is for a jet that flies at only just below the speed of sound and carries about a hundred passengers (roughly the same number as Concorde), but has the range to fly direct on long haul. Just how long a haul that could be remains the issue to be settled, with possible targets being 6000 nautical miles (Tokyo to Chicago, London to Cape Town), 7000 nm (London to Singapore, New York to Tokyo), 8000 nm (Los Angeles to Sydney, New York to Hong Kong), 9000 nm (New York to Singapore, Los Angeles to Bangkok), or even 10,000 nm, which would enable non-stop London-to-Sydney flights. Speeds of Mach 0.95 (compared to the Mach 0.8 of typical jetliners today) would mean time-savings of nearly two hours over a 7000 nm route.

Clearly we don't know yet what the range and capacity of such a craft would be, and indeed it remains to be seen if it will ever make it off the drawing board; but if it were to take to the skies it would continue to increase the traveler's range of choice of speed, luxury and economy.

One thing that the Airbus super-jumbo and the Sonic Cruiser will almost certainly share is Internet connectivity in the skies. Both Boeing and rival Tenzing Communications are looking at providing Internet speeds ranging from 56kbps (the speed of a fast modem now) and high-speed megabit bandwidth of the kind currently provided by leased lines or cable. The service will rely on satellites to which Boeing aims to link, using a surfboard-shaped antenna attached to planes. There are various technical issues to be overcome: for instance, while satellite connections allow massive download speeds, they require a separate and often much slower upload path to send data. There is also the issue of demand, not least since telephone services in the air have not proved massively popular to date, partly because of cost. Nonetheless, the service is expected to start in 2002 and a number of airlines have shown interest. Within a year or so, super-jumbo passengers may be enjoying a little high-speed surfing in the skies.

KEY LEARNING POINTS

» Space is no longer the final frontier for the fare-paying tourist, and agencies are fast arranging more extra-atmospheric tours.
» Hub airports may be bypassed in the future as fast, long-distance Sonic Cruisers transport passengers directly to their long-haul destinations.
» Biometric identification, in particular iris recognition, is set to speed up the process of checking in and boarding.
» That plane you board may well be your company's own, as fractional ownership makes the use of corporate jets a sensible option.

In Practice: Travel Success Stories

» European low-cost airlines
» High-speed trains
» Ecotourism
» The relaunch of the cruise liner.

EUROPEAN LOW-COST AIRLINES

While the US went through extensive airline deregulation back in 1978 (see Chapter 3, The Evolution of Travel), the story was not the same in Europe. Although the European national carriers (such as British Airways, Air France, and Air Italia) were no longer necessarily state-owned, they still had enormous clout right up to the end of the 1980s (and some would say to this day). This was apparent in their iron grip over routes to and from their home countries. While agreements would be struck between the big names flying from one capital to the other, it was nigh on impossible for a small, independent airline from one European country to start scheduled flights within another. Such agreements between the big players did little to encourage the opportunities for low-cost competition in the market.

By the mid-1980s, however, a new generation of businesspeople was eyeing up the short- and medium-range market in Europe, and was convinced there was room for new players and particularly for those offering cheap, no-frills travel.

Ryanair, one of the first to be set up, sought to break what it describes as "a high-fare cartel" being run between Dublin and London by the two controlling national airlines, Aer Lingus and British Airways. Ryanair protested that it could provide a service at half the price of the typical £209 return, and on May 23, 1986, it started a service with two turboprop aircraft. The fledgling airline kept its promise with an introductory fare of £94.99.

The big break, however, was not to come until 1987 when the European Commission ruled that it was time to open up the skies of Europe to low-cost competition. The EC initiated a 10-year reform process intended to allow any airline holding a valid Air Operator's Certificate to operate on any route within the European Union, whether or not that route begins or ends in the airline's home nation. It heralded an open season on airfares, albeit one that would be plagued by hurdles and hiccups for another decade.

Already easyJet was pushing into Europe in 1996 with its first service to Amsterdam from London Luton, shortly followed by its Nice and Barcelona routes. Since then easyJet has grown from a two-plane outfit flying from Luton to Scotland, to one of the most successful no-frills operations, carrying some 5.6 million passengers on 35 routes serving

16 European destinations. Likewise, Ryanair prospered with the full EU deregulation, launching services from London Stansted to Stockholm and Oslo as well as to Dublin, Paris, and Brussels, all at fares less than half the cheapest provided by the rival national carriers. By 1999 Ryanair was operating 35 routes to 11 countries and carrying almost 6 million passengers. It was also the biggest Irish airline on any of the routes it ran, proof positive of its original thinking about the possibilities of the London-to-Dublin route. Depending on when they're flying, today's travelers are likely to get fares still comparable with or even cheaper than that initial offer of £94.99 – a mark of how successful Ryanair and others have been in driving down travel costs.

It hasn't always been a simple and smooth route to lower pricing, however, and easyJet in particular, with its flamboyant owner Stelios Haji-Ioannou, has never shied from publicity in the crusade against the national carriers and their collective muscle. In 1999 in response to perceived tactical blocking by Swissair, easyJet had to reinvent itself as a charter service in order to operate between Geneva and Barcelona. The airline is required to provide accommodation, which it does in the form of a tent 60 miles outside Barcelona. By 2001 Swissair had abandoned the Geneva – Barcelona route, and easyJet was able to operate as a scheduled airline.

Go, British Airways' if-you-can't-beat-them-join-them offspring, was also to become a favorite target of easyJet's publicity, which accused the new no-frills airline of being subsidized by its larger parent. Other airlines that see the no-frills way as being a bandwagon not to miss include Virgin, which launched Virgin Express, and KLM, which relaunched its UK division as Buzz.

The secret to the new generation of cheap carriers was a realization that most air travelers were paying for a lot of things they neither needed nor wanted and would happily dispense with in return for cheaper ticket pricing.

For a start, the low-cost carriers took a leaf out of the book of Southwest Airlines in the US and focused on a very small number of profitable routes. Ryanair and easyJet also moved away from the bigger airports and out to second-tier airports, further from the city but less cluttered. Ryanair chose Stansted, and easyJet has largely made Luton its own. In part this move was forced by the national carriers' control of take-off and landing slots, but the lower charges of the less central airports and the faster turnaround times (because of lower congestion) made good economic sense. No-frills flyers also opted for direct sales so as to cut out the middleman and that extra layer of cost. They were later to go one step further and promote sales on the Web as an even more cost-efficient way of selling seats. EasyJet in particular lives up to its claim to be "the Web's most popular airline" in that it sells nearly 90% of its tickets online. In January 2001 around 86% of all easyJet's seats were sold over the Net, making easyJet one of the UK's biggest Internet retailers.

Other short cuts to profitability include ticketless travel – easyJet and rivals such as Go simply send the passenger a fax or an e-mail with a reference number. At the easyJet check-in there is no numbered seat assignment either, which means you have to get in quickly if you have a seat preference. That said, the result is much faster than the normal procedure and the planes tend to fill up in one smooth flow from one end to the other, with no hanging around in the aisles as people look for their seat numbers. The no-frills flyers usually don't provide free food or drink in the air – although, as they are quick to point out, there is no such thing as a free airline lunch. Passengers have proved much happier to pay for their food if they want it, rather than have the costs of catering buried in their ticket price. When you consider the number of jokes made at the expense of airline food, it seems an obvious thing to get rid of, particularly on short- and medium-haul flights, which are rarely more than a couple of hours long.

No catering trolleys, regional airports, or unassigned seating all add up to a short time on the ground – something that some passengers would happily pay more for. There is also a deliberately less stuffy approach to the staff, reflected in more flippant cabin announcements and more relaxed dress codes – ties are banned on easyJet, for example.

What has surprised the industry is that for all this dress-down approach and lack of perks, on a typical no-frills flight you're as likely to find yourself sitting next to a laptop-wielding businesswoman as to a family going on vacation. Checking with fellow travelers on easyJet services to Barcelona and with Go to Lisbon revealed that most were going there on business. The frequency of flights (Go flies up to eight times a day on some routes) and the no-frills approach appeal to a lot of people traveling on business, whether or not they have to pay for their own expenses. This may well prove a problem for Buzz and Go, which are competing against their own parent airlines, but it is a continuing source of delight for the pure-play cost-cutters. EasyJet and Ryanair are quick to point to the operating losses of Go, something made all the more striking by their own spectacularly profitable success, but even so it is hard to imagine the larger carriers leaving the budget market entirely to the upstart no-frills newcomers.

So far there has been only one notable casualty in the price war, when cost-cutter Debonair stopped trading, and it's not in the public interest to see any more, as the cost competition has brought with it a golden era of passenger power and cheap travel. As long as they are not being subsidized by larger parents (always the accusation leveled at Go), any new entrants would be welcomed and may yet find room in the market. While the skies above Europe are among the most crowded in the world, the situation is expected to be eased by new air traffic technology that reduces the vertical distance required between planes, and by the opening up of more of the smaller regional airports beloved of the budget airlines. Overall, the International Air Transport Association (IATA) expects that passengers on international flights traveling between the countries of Europe will grow from 176 million in 1999 to 215 million in 2003, in line with an average annual growth rate of 5.1%.

The budget airlines, however, look set to fare even better than that. A Cranfield University report published in January 2000 estimated that low-cost airlines currently carry 4% of all domestic and international passengers within Europe, a figure expected to increase to 12%–15% by 2010. The future is bright, the future is cheap, and above all the future doesn't contain shrink-wrapped salad, individual portions of cheese, non-dairy creamer, or seat numbers.

Websites for budget airlines

» easyJet: www.easyjet.co.uk (French- and Spanish-language sites also found here)
» Go: www.go-fly.com
» Ryanair: www.ryanair.com
» Virgin Express: www.virgin-express.com
» Buzz: www.buzzaway.com

Timeline

- » **1978**: The US introduces airline deregulation.
- » **1986 (May 23)**: Ryanair offers its first London-to-Dublin flight at under half the normal price.
- » **1987**: The EC initiates a 10-year plan to open European skies to competition.
- » **1995 (November)**: easyJet's inaugural flights start from London Luton to Edinburgh and Glasgow.
- » **1996**: Virgin Express launches.
- » **1996**: easyJet starts its first European service to Amsterdam from London Luton, shortly followed by flights to Nice and Barcelona.
- » **2000 (January)**: A study by Cranfield University estimates that low-cost airlines carry 4% of all domestic and international passengers within Europe.
- » **2001 (January)**: Around 86% of all easyJet's seats are sold over the Net.
- » **2010**: The low-cost airlines are expected to carry 12%–15% of domestic and international passengers within Europe.

KEY INSIGHTS

- » Big names don't mean better deals.
- » Travelers are more than happy to forgo shrink-wrapped sandwiches and assigned seating for short-haul flights.
- » Travel agents, including online booking agents such as Expedia and Travelocity, don't necessarily have the best deals for flying around Europe, because most of the low-cost airlines sell direct.
- » In the case of easyJet, ticket sales are nearly exclusively online.

THE RETURN OF THE TRAIN – EUROSTAR AND THE TGV

While no-frills flyers are making it ever cheaper to get around Europe, they are not the only means of getting from city to city. As convincing proof that you can teach an old dog new tricks, rail is emerging as the high-speed star of the new millennium.

Planes are faster than trains – there's no doubt about it. With the tumbling cost of flying, the difference between the prices of a plane ticket and a train ticket from one European capital to the next is often negligible. So who but the hard-core train enthusiast would opt to take the railcar rather than the cabin? Increasingly the answer is the business traveler, at least when it comes to trips between London, Paris, Brussels, and now Marseilles.

The breakthrough came with Eurostar, a Franco-Belgian-British consortium that came together with the aim of running French-style high-speed trains (*Trains à Grande Vitesse*, or TGVs) through the Channel Tunnel to connect the capitals.

The first Eurostar train appeared in the UK for testing in June 1993, but it wasn't until May 6, 1994, the day Queen Elizabeth II inaugurated the Channel Tunnel, that the sub-sea linkup could be tested. The first commercial service left London Waterloo International on November 14, 1994, bound for Paris Gare du Nord, shortly followed by a Brussels-bound train. The service was open, and the delights of a 300kph (186mph) train meant that the London-to-Paris service took just three hours (sadly, this speed is currently obtainable only in France). There are now 28 Eurostar departures daily serving Paris, Brussels, Lille, Bourg-St-Maurice, Moutiers, Calais, and Disneyland® Paris.

Since the flight time from London to Paris is only about an hour, it might seem that the train is the slow option. However, once you've allowed for the check-in time, the security searches, and the travel to and from the airport, it turns out in practice that the overall travel time is about the same – indeed, the train often has the edge. The only flight services that beat it are those going from City Airport in London's Docklands, which has an unmatched convenience for those working or living nearby. Even there, however, the train has the enduring advantage of traveling from city center to city center.

Once you're on the train, the journey is an uninterrupted three hours – time to fine-tune that presentation, write that report, or get stuck into the latest sex-and-shopping best-seller. By contrast the journey by air is frantic and fragmented – lost time, in fact. All of which means that the Economy Class sections of Eurostar (there is also a First Class, complete with airport-style lounge, and a Premium Economy class) are generally as full of laptops and handheld computers as they are of day-trippers. By introducing portable DVD players to rent, Eurostar has even provided the means to catch an in-journey movie, something you don't have time for on the plane.

There are catches – there are no really early morning trains, and the time difference between the UK and the rest of Europe means that the train is not really an option for getting to that first-thing meeting in Brussels on the day itself. Eurostar has also tried its best to increase its margin from business travelers by insisting on a Saturday-night stay as a qualification for cheap fares, but then the airlines have been doing that for decades. Frequent travelers find it cheaper to book an open-ended return on their way out (stipulating an open return that takes in a Saturday night), and then another on their way back, using the two return legs to provide another trip within the next couple of months. Whatever the incidental quibbles, Eurostar has meant that rail travel is back with a vengeance and that business flights have real competition between the three European capitals. Air France has now dropped its Paris-to-Brussels route.

The success of the approach meant that it was bound to expand further, and sure enough the next big blow for the airlines came in June 2001 with the opening of the *TGV Méditerranée* running from Paris to Marseilles. In many ways the TGV Med, as it's come to be known, is not so very different from the other TGV routes that have expanded across France since their conception in the 1960s. It provides a high-speed train service that is similar to Eurostar's, from the French capital to Marseilles, thereby serving both the Mediterranean coastline and the inland attractions of Provence. An 800km train journey that used to take around four-and-a-half hours has now been slashed to the magical three-hour figure. Better yet, there are no less than 17 trains a day.

But the importance of the service is not just that it links the first and second cities of the country. In order to understand the appeal of that route to the French, you only have to look up the accident report figures for the *Autoroute du soleil*, the fast road that runs along much the same route and is annually brought to a standstill by traffic as the great North – South migration takes place in August. For the British it means that it is possible to leave London in the morning and be blinking in the Mediterranean sun of the Vieux Port after only six hours of train travel. Not surprisingly the train was booked solid for the first two months only a few days after tickets went on sale.

This is good news unless you're an airline operator. Air France has said it anticipates a 25% fall in demand for flights between Paris and Marseilles. The airline has said that it will take up the challenge and try to compete with the train, which will perhaps mean cheaper flights to the south (the two biggest routes for Air France are Paris – Marseilles and Paris – Nice). Even then – and few travelers will be complaining – the evidence of Eurostar suggests that planes will have a hard battle to win back those business travelers who have learned to let the train take the strain.

Timeline

» **1993 (June)**: The first Eurostar train appears in the UK.
» **1994 (May 6)**: Queen Elizabeth II inaugurates the Channel Tunnel.
» **1994 (November 14)**: The first London-to-Paris service departs.
» **2001 (June)**: The opening of the *TGV Méditerranée* running from Paris to Marseilles.

KEY INSIGHTS

» Despite the speed advantage of plane over train, the convenience of travel between city centers is often more suited to the business traveler.
» Three hours seated in front of a table is more conducive to working en route than is a journey broken into many steps.
» High-speed trains are cutting into the speed advantages of planes.
» With a bit of luck, a plane/train price war should be about to break out.

ECOTOURISM SUCCESS STORIES

Ecotourism has proved to be one of the fastest growing areas of the travel and tourism business, so much so that there are fears it will be damaged by unscrupulous or ill-considered attempts to cash in on its popularity. Deciding what constitutes an ecotourism success story, therefore, means more than just adding up the numbers of visitors per year or the amount of profit made. Questions about sustainability and education have to be weighed up, and one of the better mechanisms for doing so is the judging procedure of the British Airways *Tourism for Tomorrow* awards. These are run with the support of the Association of British Travel Agents (ABTA), the American Society of Travel Agents (ASTA), the British Tourist Authority (BTA), and the Pacific Asia Travel Association (PATA), and highlight ecotourism efforts across the globe.

The criteria for the awards highlight best practice both for the environment and for the tourism business, since sustainable ecotourism is all about avoiding the damaging short-term thinking that ultimately degrades the planet and destroys the point of traveling to those locations. Winners are selected on the basis of a number of factors, including how well they protect the cultural and natural heritage of the location, the way they benefit the local community, and the way the impact on the environment is managed. Also taken into account are how well the importance of those factors is communicated to visitors and how the project ensures that it will be able to continue unspoiled for future generations.

One winner has been Savannah Guides (www.savannah-guides. com.au), a network of tour guides in northeastern Australia united by a common philosophy. It was set up in 1988 to give tourists an insight into the region but in such a way as to preserve it. All of the participating enterprises conduct natural or cultural interpretive tours and have to demonstrate a commitment to conservation. There's also a strong emphasis on professionalism and expertise, with two training schools conducted annually to educate participants in ecology and land management. The whole network is itself managed by a six-strong board known by the aboriginal term *Joongai*, meaning "keepers of the philosophies."

The tropical savannas account for nearly a quarter of the total land mass of Australia and stretch from Broome to Townsville. Despite their vast size and the variety of animal life and aboriginal culture the savannas contain, Savannah Guides is quick to admit that they are often seen as rather boring countryside – a place to pass through on the way to something more interesting. That perception has been successfully challenged by Savannah Guides members such as Far Out Adventures with its cultural tours of the Northern Territory; Gecko Canoeing and its wilderness river forays; Odyssey Safaris; and Outback Aussie Tours' voyages into the historical, cultural, and archaeological attractions of Queensland. Savannah Guides reports that the growing appreciation of the area's appeal has seen a near-threefold increase in tourist numbers in some parts of the region, so the importance of sustainable tourism is growing in proportion to the success of their operators.

Previous winners of a *Tourism for Tomorrow* award include the Chumbe Island Coral Park of Tanzania, the first marine park in that country and a potential example for others. The 24 hectares of Chumbe Island are uninhabited and support both a forest and a coral reef. Chumbe is only 12km from Zanzibar, the spice island which has been changed dramatically over the last few years by property development in the old quarter, Stone Town, and along the beaches of the East Coast where private beach resort complexes have mushroomed. It's a commonly voiced concern that such developments, often undertaken by private foreign investors, see the profits they make shipped out rather than enjoyed by the local community.

Chumbe has been developed specifically so that the local community benefits from ecotourism and has a vested interest in its preservation. The visitors' center has strictly limited accommodations to ensure that tourism doesn't swamp the reserve, and access times are limited and regulated by the tides so as to minimize the impact on the environment. All the tourist bungalows feature rainwater catchment and solar water heating for the same purpose. In terms of the local community, the fishermen have been retrained as park rangers and are now paid to protect the fish and fauna. Profits are re-invested in conservation schemes and education (local school children also benefit from free excursions).

Educating the local population and tourists alike is a key theme in successful ecotourism, as is providing incentives whereby flora and fauna are worth more living and thriving than they are dead. One scheme highlighted by the awards goes a step further, however, getting the tourists themselves in on the act of conservation. Imagine asking normal vacationers to pay to visit a resort, and then to spend their time there working on improving it. Unlikely? Perhaps, but certainly not impossible – as the work of Coral Cay Conservation (CCC) goes to show.

CCC has the preservation of rainforests and coral reefs as its goal, and hit upon the simple but effective idea of transforming tourism into part of the solution, rather than the problem, by engaging visitors in the day-to-day work of conservation.

CCC works together with local communities and conservation organizations. One example is in the Sulu Sea at Taytay Bay in the Philippines, where it is working with the Palawan Council for Sustainable Development to survey the coral reefs that fringe the hundreds of islands dotted throughout the Taytay area and pave the way for a full marine reserve. It's an approach that has worked in the past, as for example in Belize, where a survey of the marine life around South Water Cay led the Belizean government to designate the site as a Marine Protected Area. Every visitor to that country now pays a departure tax, which is channeled into the conservation of its forests and reefs.

Aside from its work in Belize, which won a *Tourism for Tomorrow* award, the CCC has since helped to create eight wildlife sanctuaries and marine reserves around the world. Every year hundreds of CCC volunteers make up expeditions to gain information about the planet's more delicate ecosystems, including projects currently underway at the Bay Islands of Honduras and three different sites in the Philippines.

The Bay Islands form part of the largest coral reef in the Western Hemisphere, a reef stretching from Mexico through Belize to Honduras. The islands themselves are a clutch of patches of land ranging from low islets (the "cays" from which the organization takes its name) to mountainous islands – all are surrounded by coral. Their appeal to scuba divers has led to the danger of coral being damaged by careless divers or anchoring. As well as potentially converting some of those recreational divers into conservationists, CCC aims to document exactly how much damage has been done, in order to help establish how best to preserve it.

In the Philippines, as well as participating in the Taytay Bay project mentioned above, the CCC is surveying the coastal area of the Negros Occidental – an extension of an earlier successful project that led to the establishment of the Danjugan Island marine reserve. Would-be volunteers can learn more at www.coralcay.org.

Timeline

- » **1864**: In the US, President Lincoln creates Yosemite National Park, set aside for public recreation.
- » **1960s**: It becomes apparent in many countries that the standard type of national park system, which largely worked on trying to divorce

the local people from the preserved areas, is causing problems, particularly in underdeveloped nations. The concept of ecotourism begins to grow, with an emphasis on culture and the education and economics needed for sustainability.

» **1980s**: Organizations such as Savannah Guides come into being.
» **1990s**: Ecotourism is now such big business that mainstream carriers such as British Airways are promoting it with the *Tourism for Tomorrow* Awards.

KEY INSIGHTS

» Ecotourism has to be protected from itself if the boom is to be sustained.
» Ecotourists are prepared to pay to do the work of conservation.
» Successful ecotourism has as much to do with improving the life of local communities as it has with providing an enjoyable vacation.

LOVE BOATS – THE RELAUNCH OF THE CRUISE LINER

Travel is about much more than getting from A to B, and sometimes the issues of speed and cost are largely irrelevant. Perhaps precisely because the modern world continues to get faster and more demanding, the slower and more gracious pace of cruise ships is as much in demand as ever. Travelocity (www.travelocity.com), the online booking site, claims to have seen cruise sales increase by 300% over the first four months of 2001. Travel Trade's *Annual Cruise Guide*, the industry bible, notes that its 2001/2002 edition now contains over 1000 itineraries and 90 cruise ships, compared with 200 itineraries back in 1980. With 38 new ships appearing in the *Guide*'s Newbuilds Chart, the cruising boom looks set to continue, and even the success of the film *Titanic* has done nothing to slow the growing interest in cruises.

Cruises have changed, however, since the days when deck quoits and an invitation to the captain's table were the highlights of the trip. While the tradition and formality of dressing for dinner is part of the appeal for some (Celebrity Cruises even offers butlers for those in suites), it is a turnoff for many who are used to dress-down days at work. Dinner at eight can prove restricting for those accustomed to cities that never sleep and food that ranges from Somali to sushi. The baby-boomer generation, used to aerobics classes and the gym culture, is also more likely to demand access to sports facilities that go beyond badminton and a splash pool.

All these factors have been taken fully on board by the cruise industry. Carnival Cruise Lines now features alternatives that include round-the-clock pizza and sushi bars; First European Cruises has afternoon tapas. Spas and fitness centers have become de rigueur and lines such as Holland America offer basketball, golf, tennis, and aerobics classes. Going that one step further, Royal Caribbean Cruises has introduced artificial rock-climbing walls, ice-skating rinks and shows, Oceanographic and Atmospheric Labs and even Mardi Gras-type parades. If all of that doesn't satisfy the adventurous, then off-ship excursions, once a simple matter of shopping and high-speed sightseeing, are now likely to include scuba diving, kayaking, and mountain climbing.

Itineraries are changing too to take in ports ever further off the beaten track, as today's tourist hungers for more exotic stop-offs. The extraordinary diversity of the cruise market has seen the number of itineraries multiplied five times over in the last two decades.

One of the last itineraries to develop, however, remains the home waters and ports of Cuba, a glaring omission in the otherwise wildly popular Caribbean cruising sector. Cuba became a no-go location in 1960 after Fidel Castro nationalized US interests on the island without compensation. The US replied with sanctions that effectively ruled the island out of bounds to US nationals. This is why the cruise ships that call there are those selling their cabins to European tourists. Festival Cruises, which is marketed as First European Cruises in the US, has announced that it will be using Havana as its home port in 2001 for a winter Caribbean tour marketed in Europe. However, legislation has already been proposed (although not ratified) to lift the travel ban for Americans, and the possibility of including Cuba on the cruise itinerary has eyes lighting up throughout the industry. If the ban is lifted, Havana could once again become a playground for US travelers, and the cruise business in the Caribbean will get a further fillip.

Whatever the location, the days when the most mentally taxing activity was the casino have also departed, and onboard lectures have become popular. Crystal Cruises has its "Computer University@Sea", with lecture courses in association with the Smithsonian; Norwegian Cruise Lines offers cooking classes, yoga, and economics lessons; and Silversea Cruises will educate passengers in art and architecture as well as on the finer points of bridge. Lectures on local culture have become popular as the more curious tourists take an interest in what's going on beyond their bulkheads. Almost all the major lines now feature Internet cafés, even Cunard, that most traditional of lines, and some are installing high-speed access points into the suites.

Another big change is that although cruises were once expected to be populated by dowagers and newlyweds, cruising is now a family affair with activities for all ages (and is often a chance for family members to take a welcome break from each other). Qualified child-minders and activity supervisors now feature on ships' rosters along with the engineers and sailors.

All of which just goes to illustrate the increasing diversity of travel today. At one end of the spectrum the new-millennium phenomena of Sonic Cruisers and space tourism (see Chapter 6, The State of the Art) are turning comic-book fantasy into reality, while at the same time the resurgence of the cruise liner and even the relaunch of the Zeppelin hark back to the early years of the twentieth century.

Timeline

» **1980**: Travel Trade's *Annual Cruise Guide* contains 200 itineraries.
» **2001**: That figure has risen to over 1000, with 38 new ships now on slipways, on the order books, or coming into commission.
» **2001**: Travelocity reports that sales of cruises have risen 300% in the first four months of the year.
» **2002**: Cuba to retake prime position on cruise itineraries?

KEY INSIGHTS

» The cruise industry is aware of the diversification and increasing sophistication of passengers.

» Its response has included everything from Internet cafés to climbing-walls, ice rinks, and 24-hour pizza.

» Food for the brain as well as for the body is now firmly on the menu, with a wide range of classes and lectures.

Key Concepts

» Hard and soft adventure travel
» Ecotourism
» Top ten ecotourism destinations
» Cultural travel
» Top ten cultural travel destinations
» Retro travel
» Complex travel
» Codesharing.

ADVENTURE TRAVEL – HARD AND SOFT

Adventure travel is one of the fastest-growing sectors, as more and more people decide that there is more to vacations than poolside cocktails and sunburn. The level of risk, excitement, rest, etc. vary wildly, as everyone has their own definition of what constitutes adventure travel, but the key ingredient is a great deal more active participation by the traveler. Within the travel business, adventure travel is often further broken down into two categories: hard adventure and soft adventure.

Hard adventure

Two factors distinguish hard adventure:

» the degree of risk involved; and, as a result
» the need for the adventurer to have experience in the type of activity involved.

Physical and mental fitness are important factors in hard adventure, and from an organizer's point of view insurance and damage waivers play an ever more important part. Hard-adventure travel includes technical rock climbing (i.e. with ropes, etc.), Class V+ river rafting, hang gliding, whitewater kayaking, survival courses, and scuba diving in cold water and strong currents.

Soft adventure

Soft adventure can be a bit of a misnomer, since there is often no shortage of sweat and adrenaline. Soft adventure is for those who want to get involved in activities but may be trying them out for the first time, or are opting to avoid the physical and mental extremes of hard-adventure travel. Soft adventure includes hiking/trekking, canoeing, horse riding, much mountain biking, sailing, and safaris. It can also include scuba-diving courses for beginners and appropriately supervised climbing and rappelling (abseiling), at which point the dividing line between soft and hard adventure comes down to experience required rather than effort expected.

ECOTOURISM

The International Ecotourism Society (www.ecotourism.org) defines ecotourism as "responsible travel to natural areas that conserves the environment and sustains the well-being of local people." Ecotourism means more than charging off to see an Amazonian rainforest before it disappears; it means helping to ensure that you as a traveler are part of the solution, not the problem. Environmentally responsible travel stresses not just the immediate natural environment of a region, but also the culture and well-being of local individuals and economies. That in turn means looking into the impact of the tourist dollar – who is on the receiving end of it? Does it help toward a sustainable industry or lead to a "robber" industry that will eventually degrade the area being visited?

Ironically, the fact that ecotourism is such a growth area has led to the tag being appropriated by any number of ill-thought-out schemes and blatant attempts to cash in with little or no real regard for the environment. Wrongly labeled "ecotourism" is one of the problems as travel goes increasingly global. Eugenio Yunis, the World Tourism Organization's Chief of Sustainable Development of Tourism, warns, "Unsustainable ecotourism is putting at risk the survival of the natural environment that is the very bedrock of the ecotourism business and, more serious still, detracts from and even discredits this activity." 2002 has been designated as the International Year of Ecotourism in a bid to raise awareness of the issues at stake.

Ecotravel (www.ecotravel.com), an online ecotravel magazine, proposes the following questions for any ecotraveler planning a trip.

» Is the destination overcrowded or overdeveloped?
» Is the tour operator or guide aware of environmental concerns?
» Does the tour operator or guide contribute financially to conservation and preservation efforts?
» Are the accommodations environmentally sensitive?
» Are there any advisories, rules, or regulations regarding protected areas, water sources, or wildlife habitats?
» What behavior is appropriate when viewing wildlife?
» Will the trip support the work of conservation and preservation organizations?

The fact that a trip is focused on flora and fauna does not in itself make it an ecofriendly one. There are too many examples of cowboy companies offering tourists the "once in a lifetime" chance to hunt, collect eggs, or chop trees in ecologically sensitive environments.

Such offers should not only be declined, they should be complained about and publicized, since ecotourism is one of the fastest growing areas of travel and unless it is managed sensibly it will only serve to destroy the thing it loves. More checklists and guidelines are at www.bigvolcano.com.au/natural/nattract.htm#ecotourists.

If you're looking for further ideas for ecotravel, take a peek at Concierge.com, the Website for Condé Nast Traveler. In conjunction with adventure specialists iExplore and the *National Geographic*, it lists a top ten of the most popular ecotravel destinations in the world. At the time of writing, it goes like this.

1. **Manu National Forest, Peru**. Jaguars, macaws, and caiman are among the attractions in this rainforest, which is replete with canopy platforms for viewing the monkeys and bird life of the treetops.
2. **Bwindi Impenetrable National Park, Uganda**. The name gives a hint as to the continued survival of this site, home to nearly half the world's population of mountain gorillas, and the best place to see them in the light of troubles in Rwanda.
3. **Fraser Island, Australia**. Listed as a World Heritage site, this island off the coast of Queensland manages to combine rainforest and sandy beaches with a diversity of wildlife to match, including 250 species of birds.
4. **Talamanca Range – La Amistad Reserves, Costa Rica and Panama**. This convergence point of two continents (North and South America) and two oceans (Pacific and Atlantic) has a biodiversity to live up to its billing.
5. **Mount Cook National Park, New Zealand**. Glaciers and thermal pools are side by side in this rainforested mountain on South Island.
6. **Sepik River, Papua New Guinea**. Carvings, totems, ancestral houses, and wildlife that's still being discovered and classified.
7. **Hoh Rainforest, Olympic National Park, Washington, USA**. Homegrown rainforest replete with 500-year-old trees.
8. **Kakum National Park, Ghana**. A walkway 25m up in the air is just one of the attractions of this ancient forest, where ecotourism is being promoted as an alternative to the timber trade in an attempt to preserve the area's attractions.
9. **Batang Ai National Park, Malaysia**. On the island of Borneo in the territory of Sarawak, Batang Ai is one of the last homes to

the orangutan, that most gentle of great apes. As orangutans are increasingly rare in the wild and shy by nature, a sighting is not guaranteed, although one is all the more precious for that. Those deprived of the chance to see the apes in the wild can always visit the Semenggok Wildlife Rehabilitation Center, where the orphaned or injured are rehabilitated prior to release.

10 **Tikal National Park, Guatemala**. This is a Mayan ceremonial center in the heart of the jungle.

CULTURAL TRAVEL

Technically, anywhere you travel that has inhabitants could be classed as a cultural destination, and some would argue, with good reason, that a trip to Blackpool or Las Vegas is as much a plunge into human culture as strolling around the Musée d'Orsay or Pompeii. Since time immemorial, however, there has been a cachet to certain cultural sites, whether they be the Seven Wonders of the Ancient World, or the European cultural hotspots of the nineteenth century "grand tour" for gentlemen of leisure. The locations themselves have changed, not least since almost all of the Seven Wonders have disappeared. Just as a reminder, the original cultural hit parade ran as follows.

Seven Wonders of the Ancient World

» The Great Pyramid at Giza in Egypt
» The Hanging Gardens of Babylon
» The Temple of Artemis at Ephesus
» The Statue of Zeus at Olympia
» The Mausoleum at Halicarnassus
» The Colossus of Rhodes
» The Lighthouse of Alexandria.

By the time of the Middle Ages there was a new list, partly thanks to the destruction of some of the above, partly because of the expansion of the known world to include China.

Seven Wonders of the Middle Ages

» The Coliseum of Rome
» The Catacombs of Alexandria
» The Great Wall of China

» The Leaning Tower of Pisa
» The Porcelain Tower of Nanking
» The Mosque of St Sophia at Constantinople
» Stonehenge.

One of the differences between the wish lists of the Seven Wonders era and modern times is that very few travelers of any era would ever have seen all seven. The relative ease of modern travel means that the restless traveler will have seen many if not most of the most popular cultural icons (the Eiffel Tower, Sydney Harbor Bridge, the Statue of Liberty, etc.), which have acquired a mainstream, even kitsch, association. Of course the great palaces and art museums of the world still retain their appeal, with their ranks swelled by recent additions such as the Guggenheim Museum in Bilbao, Spain, or the Tate Modern at Bankside, London.

The accessibility of these, however, means they will always have slightly less kudos than is given to a more arcane cultural heritage, perhaps buried in an offbeat location. "Cultural travel" now is taken to mean a slightly more eclectic range of less obvious archaeological treasures. It's not that they are necessarily more or less worthy than the more mainstream tourist destinations, but just that they have that elusive cachet. For today's cultural traveler, Condé Nast lists the following as the top ten countdown to cultural heaven. Updated listings can be found at www.concierge.com.

1 **Terra-Cotta Army, Xi'an, China**. Possibly the greatest archaeological discovery of the twentieth century, this legion of clay warriors features life-size soldiers, horses, and carriages in terra-cotta, all guarding the tomb of Emperor Qin Shi Huang.

2 **Pyramids and Sphinx, Giza, Egypt**. The only survivor of the original Seven Wonders still to be found on the tourist itinerary, the appearance of the Great Pyramid with the other Pyramids and the Sphinx in the top ten is testament to their enduring appeal.

3 **Newgrange, Boyne Valley, Ireland**. Definitely one for the culture connoisseur, Newgrange, an Irish circle of engraved standing stones, predates both the pyramids and Stonehenge, without the fame or flocks of package tourists.

4 **Angkor, Cambodia**. The Dead Kennedys once sang of a *Holiday in Cambodia*; now that the country has more or less shaken off the nightmare memories of the Khmer Rouge era, it is once again celebrating the ancient Khmer empire and with it the Angkor Wat, most famous of all its temples.

5 **Petra, Wadi Musa Canyon, Jordan**. Deep in Indiana Jones territory here, Petra is the archaeological jewel of the Middle East. Most travelers still opt to venture on horseback through the narrow cliff gaps that open up to reveal a breathtaking city carved into the stone.

6 **Machu Picchu, Peru**. Like the pyramids, this suffers a little from the advent of mass tourism but is still sufficiently awe-inspiring to be worth shouldering your way through to witness the great Inca city.

7 **Calakmul, Yucatan, Mexico**. 50m-tall buildings, and the 1200-year-old mummified body of a Mayan ruler.

8 **Tombouctou, Mali**. Forbidden to western travelers, Tombouctou or Timbuktu was a center of Islamic power and a key step on the trade route for trans-Saharan caravans carrying salt and other goods. Because its exact whereabouts were unknown and because in any case it was out of bounds for white men, Timbuktu achieved a mythical status, being rumored to be built of gold and jewels. In 1828 the French explorer René Caillée finally made it there and found it to be a drab, wind-buffeted, fly-blown place. He was largely disbelieved, such was the romance attached to the name, and it took a large number of subsequent travelers (including the author) to confirm that it is indeed but a shadow of the dream. Worth a detour, as the French would say, if not a journey, although the cachet remains considerable.

9 **Acropolis, Athens, Greece**. The Acropolis somehow failed to make it into the Seven Wonders list despite being in existence from 447 BC and being one of the world's most recognizable monuments. The high city features such fabulous buildings as the Parthenon, but of course remains stripped of much of its marble decoration, that having been whisked back to England (and the British Museum) by Lord Elgin.

10 **Cliff Palace, Mesa Verde National Park, Colorado, USA**. The cliffs and canyons are fairly liberally scattered with ruins, but the

Cliff Palace stands out as the largest and best known of the Mesa Verde pueblos, featuring 150 rooms, towers, and courtyards. The story goes that it was lost for half a millennium, before being found by farmers in search of lost cattle.

Culturally sustainable tourism

Taking a look at the cultural destinations above, it is clear that over the years their reputations change constantly, going in and out of fashion. One day there will be T-shirts saying "My parents went to Shibam in the Wadi Hadramaut and all I got was this lousy T-shirt." That may be part of the natural cycle of travel and tourism, and one that such relatively well run spots as those above can afford. The near limitless reach of transport now, however, means that quite a lot of travel, be it cultural, eco, or adventure, is specifically undertaken in places that remain little changed by mass tourism. The "unspoilt" location is a mainstay of everyone's travel yarns.

The catch-22 is that by visiting such places it is hard not to contribute to their decline. This is not simply an ecological issue affecting flora and fauna. Despite the impression given by "culture travel", culture is not restricted to dead societies, and travel and tourism have an immense impact on the host culture. It is often a negative impact, and while tour operators have been accused of a slash-and-burn mentality towards location or social degradation, there is a growing feeling that sustainable tourism is possible even in remote areas, if local people are included in the rewards.

Some destinations feel this so keenly that they are implementing legislation to avoid the negative effects of tourism. In Gambia, for example, there have long been tourist resorts along the white sand beaches of the coast. The visitors, however, remained entirely within their resorts, save for organized bus trips to select spots inland, such as the birthplace of Kunta Kinte, the principal character of Alex Hailey's *Roots*. No products were bought from locals, and no money flowed to local attractions. The only cultural benefit came from begging at the gates of the resorts, or to those who conducted holiday flings with visiting tourists and received presents in return (this actually contributed surprising amounts to the local economy in the 1980s). The government in Banjul has since banned all-inclusive vacations, precisely so that visitors are encouraged to explore (and spend) further in the local economy, but it took years to get to this point.

Many cultures and economies are not so surefooted in their dealings with tourists, and sustainable tourism thinking says that it is therefore down to tourists to ask themselves whether they are part of the problem or the solution. Ecotravel.com proposes the following questions to help decide.

Questions you can ask to help preserve the culture

» Are the tour operator and accommodations sensitive to the local culture?

» What are the host country's customs? Remember that you are a guest and behave accordingly.

» What are the local conventions with regard to dress?

» Where, how, and when should you take photographs? Always ask first.

» How well do you know the language? Speaking to local people in their language demonstrates your respect for their culture.

» Are there any local cultural events? Your support helps local performers preserve their heritage.

» How does tourism impact the local culture?

Questions you can ask to help sustain local economies

» Are the lodges, hotels, tour guides, and transportation services locally owned and operated?

» Do the tour company and accommodations employ local people and purchase local products?

» Where are the local restaurants and local markets?

» Are the souvenirs you purchase made by local craftspeople and artisans?

» Are there access fees to protected sites? Your money supports local efforts to conserve those areas.

» What is a fair price for the goods or services offered by the local people? You should make every effort to offer a fair price. (More than 80% of travelers' fees from most all-inclusive package tours go to airlines, hotels, and other companies that are not locally owned.)

RETRO TRAVEL

Although travel is a fast-forward business and travel technology is supposedly shrinking the planet, there will always be a hankering after a different approach and pace. Since many people travel for escape, the idea of escaping back in time means that any loss of speed during the journey becomes a bonus, not a drawback. The desire for retro travel is often allied to luxury, partly as a feature of nostalgia, partly as a nod to the need for profit margins despite operating more demanding machinery. Hence, for example, the reintroduction of the restored vintage luxury carriages on the Orient Express train route. Other examples of retro travel include the relaunch of Zeppelin airships in Germany or Delta Queen Coastal Voyages (a subsidiary of American Classic Voyages Company), which operates cruises on ships designed to resemble the coastal packet ships of the 1800s.

COMPLEX TRAVEL

Complex travel simply recognizes the fact that not all travelers were created the same. Areas that were once considered niche tourism (such as ecotours or adventure sports) have been seen to grow and become mainstream but are still relatively mass-market. So-called complex travel is the business of delving further into as yet relatively unexploited niches and catering for the very specific needs of individuals. Complex travel services might include catering for dietary, religious, or handicap requirements. Even smokers now come under the category of complex travel in an age of non-smoking hotels, planes, trains, and restaurants. What makes complex travel a feasible business niche is the growth of technology, particularly the Internet, meaning that even a small agency can now poll any number of different travel suppliers via the Web to put together an agenda for even the most demanding of individuals.

CODESHARING

Codesharing agreements enable a ticketing airline to issue tickets on another operating airline and to use that airline's two-letter code when doing so. A codesharing agreement can be between a larger airline and a regional airline or between a US airline and a foreign airline, and theoretically allows separate airlines to offer coordinated services including connecting flights and Air Miles share-outs. It should not be confused with interlining, which simply meant that one airline that didn't serve a final destination passed passengers on to another that did (regardless of frequent-flyer tie-ins or directly connecting flight times). Where codesharing has found itself a source of controversy is from the belief that ever-stronger alliances between rival airline blocs is effectively cutting down competition in the airline market.

Resources

» Websites for online booking, information, and travel tips
» Books for the Express Exec.

AIR TRAVEL AND SELECTING A TRIP

» **EasyJet** (www.easyjet.com) Pioneer of the no-frills approach to short- and medium-hop European travel. EasyJet is also one of the forerunners of ticketless travel and online booking, with over 80% of its flights sold on the Web.

» **Ryanair** (www.ryanair.com) Like easyJet, Ryanair is a cut-price carrier flying from the UK and Ireland to the rest of Europe. As well as being a well-established first port of call for all Irish expats looking for a flight home, it has become a favorite with opportunists, thanks to its incredible promotions, which can see flights on offer for less than £10 (excluding tax). Such madness doesn't seem to have stopped Ryanair becoming one of the most profitable of all the no-frills outfits.

» **Lastminute.com** (www.lastminute.com) Over-hyped, over-exposed, and a byword for dotcom mania but while many people are sick of its name, it is still worth a look for last-minute impulse travel, as well as gifts, tickets, etc. The new adults-only section means that this is one of the few sites where you can book yourself a break and also buy an inflatable husband or wife to go with you.

» **Expedia** (www.expedia.com – www.expedia.co.uk in the UK) Born out of software giant Microsoft, Expedia gives instant access to thousands of flights, car rental deals, and hotels, usually with detailed city maps to help you hit the ground running when you do arrive at your destination.

» **Priceline** (www.priceline.com – www.priceline.co.uk in the UK) The idea behind Priceline is simple – you just say how much you want to pay for your trip and it works out whether there is a way of making it happen. Clearly this is not for those with rigid ideas about which carriers to fly with, or even with specific destinations in mind, but for the flexible traveler it can be a great money-saver.

» **Ebookers** (www.ebookers.com) One of the most popular travel sites in the UK, not least for an extensive database of some of the lowest prices available. In August 2000 it generated 25% more hits than the UK number two, Thomas Cook.

» **Thomas Cook** (www.thomascook.com) The pioneer in traditional travel that also became one of the very first sites to sell vacations online in 1995.

» **Bargain Holidays** (www.bargainholidays.com) Exactly what it sounds like, specializing in late-availability deals.

LOCATION GUIDES

» **Resorts Online** (www.resortsonline.com) A US-based site catering for the better-heeled traveler in search of casinos, golfing, and five-star resorts generally.

» **Cityvox** (www.cityvox.com) Multilingual travel guide to over 40 European cities.

» **Time Out** (www.timeout.com) The *Time Out* city guides have now grown into one of the best online resources for travelers – restaurants, hotels, things to do, places for the kids, you name it.

» **Concierge** (www.concierge.com) Travel supersite incorporating Condé Nast Traveler. It includes airfares and vacations for sale, but its real strength is the content covering destinations, activities, and new ideas.

» **Fodor's** (www.fodors.com) Excellent hotel and restaurant index, an extensive travel forum where travelers can swap notes, and a wide range of features and articles.

» **Lonely Planet** (www.lonelyplanet.com) The bible of the backpacker, Lonely Planet's dog-eared pages can be found peeking out from the rucksacks of independent travelers the planet over. The Website, if less of an essential companion, is nonetheless a good guide to ideas and destinations for the more intrepid and/or less well-heeled.

SPECIAL TRAVEL

» **Ecotravel Magazine** (www.ecotravel.com) Articles and advice for the conscientious adventurer.

» **Big Volcano** (www.bigvolcano.com.au/ercentre/ercpage.htm) Excellent resource site for ecotourism codes of practice, news, and associations.

» **Specialty Travel** (www.specialtytravel.com) Shakespearean holidays, trips to Antarctica, ecotours, you name it.

» **Bare Necessities** (www.bare-necessities.com) Nudist vacations – "relaxing, entertaining and health-conscious vacation opportunities" with no clothes on.

TRAVEL NEWS AND ADVICE

» **CNN travel section** (www.cnn.com/travel) Travel news and features.

» **Foreign and Commonwealth Office Travel Advice** (www.fco.gov.uk/travel) Official UK government advice for British citizens traveling abroad, with an eye to keeping travelers out of trouble. Coups, lawlessness, natural disasters, anti-British demonstrations, and outbreaks of disease are (theoretically) signaled here along with travel advice notices and consular information. If you are traveling to a dangerous location, this is particularly useful, as it recommends that you contact the British Consul on arrival and departure.

» **US State Department travel section** (www.state.gov/travel.cfm).

» **Medicine Planet** (travelhealth.com/public) For medical advice before you go.

» **Virtual Tourist** (www.virtualtourist.com) Offers information on tourism around the world, based on the experiences of over 90,000 members.

CAR RENTAL

» **Alamo** (www.freeways.com)
» **Avis** (www.avis.com)
» **Budget** (www.drivebudget.com)
» **Dollar** (www.dollar.co.uk)
» **Europcar** (www.europcar.com)
» **Hertz** (www.hertz.com)
» **National** (www.nationalcar-europe.com)
» **Rent-a-Wreck of America** (www.rent-a-wreck.com)
» **Thrifty** (www.thrifty.com).

TRAIN TRAVEL

» **Travelocity Train Travel** (travelocityx.raileurope.com/us/rail/about_train_travel) Includes information not only on the many different national services, but also on the different rail cards and passes to get the best deal for national or international travel while on vacation.

» **UK Public Transport Information** (www.pti.org.uk) This directory of travel indexes, timetables, and ticket offices actually goes beyond trains to include flights and even ferries for the UK.

» **European Rail System** (www.starnetic.com/eurorail/railindx.htm) More information on Eurorail passes and tips on train travel.
» **VI Rail – Canada's Passenger Train Network** (www.virail.ca).
» **Amtrak** (www.amtrak.com) US train authority.
» **Trainline** (www.thetrainline.com) Booking service for UK trains.
» **Eurotunnel** (www.eurotunnel.com) The company that takes care of the Tunnel itself and the trains that shuttle cars through it.
» **Eurostar** (www.eurostar.com) Connecting Paris, Brussels, and London at high speed.
» **World Wide Events** (wwevents.com) The place to go to find out about wild and wonderful events around the world. Ever wanted to see the Hanagasa Matsuri Floral Sedge-Hat Festival in Yamagata City, Japan? Course you have.

BUSINESS TRAVEL

» **Worldbiz Business Cultures worldwide** (www.worldbiz.com) Country-by-country business cultures, practices, and protocols.
» **Business Travel Net** (www.business-travel-net.com) Airlines, hotels, car rental companies, and a whole host of other business-travel products and services.
» **InsideFlyer** (www.insideflyer.com) *InsideFlyer* is the magazine that frequent travelers turn to for time-sensitive airline, hotel, car rental, and affinity credit card program information. Dedicated solely to frequent travelers and their many free award programs, *InsideFlyer* provides news and information that can be found nowhere else in the world.
» **USA Today Business Travel Guide** (www.usatoday.com/life/travel/business/ltb000.htm) News affecting business travel, and a variety of articles on tips and tricks.
» **About Business Travel** (businesstravel.about.com/mbody.htm) Covers a wide scope – everything from tipping to airline seat maps and corporate compensation for life on the road.
» **Business Travel News Online** (www.btnonline.com) As its name suggests. It includes hotel and airline deals.
» **Book a seat on a private jet** (www.privateseats.com) The "Private Seats" program has been operating flights between Atlanta and New York City out of alternative airports on corporate jets since April

2000. Scheduled corporate jets offer the traveling public a new way to travel without encountering the hassle of large airports and the associated long delays, herds of people, and limited service. Private Seats provides a first-class environment and personal service without your having to charter an entire corporate aircraft. Seats are sold directly to the public via a charter/operator. Additional city pairs will begin operating in the first quarter of 2001. Costs are higher than for first class.

MISCELLANEOUS

» **Help for World Travelers** (www.kropla.com) Planning an international trip? Take a look at this site before you go, and print it off for use in an emergency. This is simply the Web's most comprehensive listing of worldwide electrical and telephone information, including international dialing codes, electricity supply information, and a world phone guide. Everything you could want to know about getting online from a strange hotel room is to be found at www.kropla.com/phones.htm. Advice on everything from ''tax impulse'' signals (used to meter calls) that are interfering with your data, through basic wire tapping, to acoustic couplers – anything and everything you could need to know in order to hook up. With the data on this site you can get online from just about anywhere.

» **The Universal Currency Converter** (www.xe.net/currency) The Universal Currency Converter claims to be the world's most popular currency tool, allowing interactive foreign exchange rate calculations on the Internet, using live, up-to-the-minute currency rates.

» **Pet Friendly Travel** (www.pet-friendly-travel.com) ''No need to leave an important family member home,'' explains this site, ''when hundreds of vacation condos, resorts, inns, bed and breakfasts, motels and hotels welcome your pet.''

» **AirlinesSuck** (www.airlinessuck.com) The name says it all, really. While it's impossible to know to what extent the airline business takes note of Airlines Suck it is nonetheless a great place to blow off steam about any and all varieties of shoddy treatment endured at the hands of the airlines. Individual hate sites can also be found dedicated to specific airlines such as www.untied.com (United), or www.northworstair.org (Northwest).

» **Skyrage Foundation** (www.skyrage.org) Not actually a complaint site at all, but rather geared towards awareness of the phenomenon of sky rage – those outbursts of antisocial behavior and violence that occur when you cram a couple of hundred people into an oversize cigar tube, pump them full of free alcohol, and take them 10km up in the air.

FINDING A CYBERCAFÉ AT YOUR TARGET DESTINATION

Going to be out of the country/continent for a few days? You might want to take a laptop and log on, but if you just want to check your e-mail occasionally then a cybercafé may be all you need. There are books that list cybercafés, but these are rarely very extensive and inevitably date badly, so that cafés have shut or moved even before publication. Try a dedicated cybercafé search engine instead.

» **Cybercafe.com** (www.cybercafe.com) Cybercafe.com is a search engine to help you find out where to go to log on before you arrive in that strange city. At the time of writing, this site contains a database of 4193 Internet cafés in 148 countries, but new ones are added all the time and you can recommend ones you know. You can search by city or by country name, or click on a map for quick access to regional listings. Listings include location (country, city, address), home page URL, and e-mail address.
» **Cybercaptive** (cybercaptive.com) This too is a search engine for finding those elusive public access points, and one which claims (as of June 2001) database listings for 6739 verified cybercafés, public Internet access points, and kiosks, in 167 countries.

WHERE TO COMPLAIN (IN THE US) WHEN IT ALL GOES WRONG

» **Better Business Bureau Online Complaint System** (www.bbb. org/bbbcomplaints/Welcome.asp) This acts as a middleman between the outraged and the airlines by forwarding complaints to the companies concerned. It also notes details of unresolved complaints and has a file of frequent offenders. Because of that, not only should it be carbon-copied on any complaints, but it also acts as a reference site to check whether the airline or travel company has a record of previous poor behavior.

» **Transportation Department's Monthly Air Travel Consumer Report** (www.dot.gov/airconsumer) For those unsure whether they have a legitimate grievance, or who don't really know how to go about complaining to a company, this site is there to help as well as to provide a tally of statistics on air travel problems.

» **Federal Trade Commission Consumer Protection** (www.ftc.gov/bcp/menu-travel.htm) While not specifically about travel, this site has useful advice on such related areas as timeshare fraud, telemarketing travel scams, and e-mail fraud. Unlike the Better Business Bureau, the FTC is not there to act as a middleman in complaints with airlines or travel companies, *but it does. . .*

» **Aviation Consumer Action Project** (www.acap1971.org) Founded by Ralph Nader in 1971, it accepts consumer complaints to help it promote consumer rights "through public advocacy, research, policy statements, and testifying before Congress and administrative agencies."

» **EComplaints** (www.ecomplaints.com) This is a broad-ranging complaint site from the Big Apple with a travel section that covers everything from car rental to hotels. As well as firing off your own malcontent missives, you can also rate companies on the site, read the grudges of others and catch up with the eComplaints top ten of the most complained-about companies.

» **PlanetFeedback** (www.planetfeedback.com) "Ticked off or tickled about holiday travel?" the home page says. "Sound off here!" Despite that militant call, the site solicits compliments as well as complaints. Travel is only one of the many areas it covers. Based in Cincinnati, it uses the Internet to help consumers gain satisfaction by helping them to be heard. Consumer input is fed into a database that rates businesses, good and bad.

» **PassengerRights** (www.passengerrights.com) The founders, Randy Warren and Michael Gross, say they hoped "to revolutionize and revive a once glamorous [travel] industry." Complaints filed online are forwarded to the target companies and to such high-and-mighties as the President of the United States, the First Lady, the Transportation Department, and Senator John McCain's Committee on Commerce, Science and Transportation. Thirty-nine "horror stories" are displayed.

» **About.com Guide to Air Travel** (www.airtravel.about.com) Click on "Complaints" on the left side of the home page and you'll learn where to find a wide variety of information on and help with travel problems. Complaints may be filed online and will be added to their "growing statistical database which may be of interest to the airlines and the government agencies that oversee/regulate the airline industry."

BOOKS

The sheer volume of travel books on the market, combined with the many personal ideas of what travel is about, means that it is impossible to make a meaningful selection of all the travelogues and guides. The following can only therefore be a taster of some books likely to appeal to the wandering Express Exec.

» Randy Petersen - *The Official Frequent Flyer Guidebook*. Airpress (ISBN 1882994051). The bible of the frequent flyer.

» Roger Collis and Kogan Page - *The Survivor's Guide to Business Travel*. International Herald Tribune. A collection of business travel columns from the *IHT*. Eurocentric but with a widely-applicable commonsense basis.

» Ronni Eisenberg and Kate Kelly - *Organize Your Business Travel: Simple routines for managing your work when you're out of the office*. Hyperion (ISBN 0786886269). Because life must go on while you're away, and you don't want a trip spoilt by fear of what exactly you're coming back to.

» Christopher J. McGinnis - *The Unofficial Business Traveler's Pocket Guide: 165 tips even the best business traveller may not know*. McGraw-Hill (ISBN 0070453802).

» James Fallows - *Free Flight: From airline hell to a new age of travel*. Public Affairs (ISBN 1586480405). A vision of the future in which the use of smaller planes flying faster and direct avoids the nightmares of mass travel and hub airports. Music to the ears of the Boeing design team working on the Sonic Cruiser.

» Martin Mowforth and Ian Munt – *Tourism and Sustainability: New tourism in the Third World*. Routledge (ISBN 0415137640). A somewhat academic guide to sustainable tourism and how it can be a bonus for underdeveloped countries.

» Ronald L. Krannich and Caryl Rae Krannich – *Jobs for People Who Love to Travel: Opportunities at home and abroad*. Impact Publications (ISBN 1570231141). Ideas for those business travelers for whom the travel comes first.

» Robert E. Bauman – *The Complete Guide to Offshore Residency, Dual Citizenship and Second Passports*. The Sovereign Society (ISBN 1903590043). Expensive at just under $100, but the guide for those taking business travel to its extreme.

Ten Steps to Making Travel Work

» Forward planning
» Essential preparation
» Avoiding classic hurdles
» Ensuring you can get your job done
» Making sure you get the best rate
» Making sure you don't end up personally out of pocket.

Here's how to put together the perfect trip.

1. DO YOUR RESEARCH BEFORE YOU GO

These days there are so many guidebooks, online city maps, travel Websites and bulletin boards that there is no excuse for not knowing a little about your destination (see Chapter 9, Resources). Yet we all still turn up in unfamiliar locations and realize we have very little time and even less of an idea of what it was we wanted to get from a place. Frequently this is because we take for granted that because it's only another European or American city, or a country whose people speak the same language as we do, then it will be easy to get our bearings and find our way around. Sadly, that is rarely true, and many of us will barely scrape the surface of our destinations, when with a few words to the wise we could have uncovered its gems.

2. DO YOUR PRE-TRAVEL PREPARATION

Language, health, and insurance are all things that need to be sorted out well before embarking on the plane. For the first of these, bear in mind that while it may be too much to ask for you to pick up fluent Tagalog for that weekend trip, nonetheless a few words and simple phrases will ease your way anywhere in the world. People of every nation appreciate a visitor's effort in speaking a few phrases, and some are notorious for their disinclination to help those who haven't made such an effort. If you've ever witnessed the studied contempt of Parisian waiters for those tourists without a word of French, you will appreciate the rewards of spending some time with a phrasebook or an online pronunciation guide.

When it comes to health, bear in mind that diseases such as malaria are reckoned to be affecting tourists more and more because of simple complacency. Either we don't take our preventative pills, or we stop taking them as soon as we get home, when in fact the full course should continue for weeks after our return. In terms of forward planning, bear in mind that some vaccinations effectively cancel each other out if taken at the same time, and so you may require days or weeks between one and the next.

Finally, don't forget that one of the most important health precautions you can take is to ensure you have full insurance to cover all eventualities, including helicopter ambulances and get-you-home-in-a-hurry repatriation. If planning on adventure activities, check the small print of your insurance. Some policies will exclude skiing, while others will allow scuba, for example, but with the proviso that insurance is invalid beyond a certain (usually very shallow) depth. That almost certainly means that your insurer will decline responsibility for any decompression-related sickness, including the cost of treatment involving pressure chambers.

3. CONSIDER WHAT YOU NEED TO KNOW WHEN YOU ARRIVE

When you arrive at your destination, it's often late at night, and you're at your most tired and disorientated. Airports are a dream location for rip-offs of all kinds, and anyway you simply don't want to be queuing for tourist information or money-changing when you've just spent half an hour getting through Immigration and chasing down your luggage.

For a start, see if you can be met at the airport – a friendly face or your name on a signboard goes a long way to easing your way into a new country. If you don't know anyone in the country, or there is no local office prepared to meet you, have you asked your hotel if they can pick you up? If you intend to collect a rental car at the airport, ensure that you have confirmed your reservation, and find out if the desk is in the terminal at which you arrive and whether or not it will be manned. If it is unmanned, where will the keys be? Airport rental desks usually charge a good deal more than if you go into town and pick up a car from a local company, but you may prefer the convenience of transportation there and then. Make sure you have booked ahead, though, or you will have to rely on elbowing your way to the front.

If you're neither being met nor renting a car, do you know what a local licensed taxi looks like? Are the taxis metered? If not, or if the meters aren't a reliable guide, do you know what the cost of your trip should be? Some online booking sites such as Expedia try to give that information, but the surest way is usually to ask a friend or colleague who has been there, or else to ask the tourist information service before you leave. If you forget that, then try the cabin staff before you land, as they will often have a pretty shrewd idea of the dos and don'ts on arrival.

Make sure you know in advance how much you should tip, and ensure that you have enough local currency for the purpose in small-denomination notes or coins. Having to break out a large note at the dead of night is at best an invitation to a long wait for change.

If taxis are beyond your budget, you need to know in advance if there is a shuttle train or bus to the city center and how long it will take. Don't simply rely on it being obvious when you get there, as you may find yourself faced with instructions or choices that are less than obvious. A new arrival at Heathrow, for example, may see little difference between the subterranean Heathrow Express and the London Underground tube line. In terms of price and time taken, the difference is considerable, but you won't want to research that *in situ* by hauling yourself and your luggage from one to the other.

4. CHOOSE YOUR TRAVEL AGENT (IF ANY) WITH CARE

Much of the travel agent's traditional task has been largely usurped by the Web – there's little point getting someone else to go through screens of flights and prices when you can do it yourself and fine-tune a trip to fit your budget and itinerary. However, that doesn't mean that travel agents are redundant, only that they have to work a little harder to justify their existence – which is an excellent thing (unless, dear reader, you are yourself a travel agent).

In the first instance, online travel sites such as Expedia and Travelocity are rarely without bias, simply because they are linked to certain airline reservation systems. The same is true of most travel agents, incidentally, but since they aren't all linked to the same system you may miss out by remaining fiercely loyal to any one solution. For flights to Africa I personally find that one particular London travel agency has consistently come up with better pricing than any of the online booking sites, although the mainstream routes (transatlantic and continental Europe) are usually cheaper online. The rule seems to be that if your needs are in any way "niche", whether in terms of destination, diet, or desired itinerary, then it will almost certainly be in your interest to look for a specialist, or for someone unusually tireless in the search for what you want.

5. CONSIDER MONEY

It may seem obvious, but the issue of how you are going to pay could make or break a trip. Simply producing the plastic may not cut it in some countries: France and Germany, for example, do not have the credit-card culture of the US or the UK. Where establishments take plastic in France it is likely to be Visa rather than Mastercard, with American Express coming way down the list.

Traveler's checks may be the safe way to carry money, but they depend on your finding somewhere to cash them, and you can bet your bottom traveler's check that there will be an obscure religious holiday the minute you need to find a bank to do the job for you. Make sure your traveler's checks will be recognized, too; a friend of mine who worked for Thomas Cook was mortified to find that the original issuer of traveler's checks was completely unheard of where she was taking her vacation. She eventually cashed the checks but only after being treated as if she was trying to pass off fake currency.

Probably the easiest way these days is to rely on cash machines (ATMs) – but again find out in advance if your card system will work at your destination and if so in which banks. It's also worth noting that some countries don't expect a high level of efficiency from their cash machines. I remember a spell in Venezuela in which machines would pay out only sporadically (because of an unreliable computer connection), so you got into the habit of looking for a queue at the machines and joining it whenever you saw one. It is always more risky to take your own cash, other than a small amount of local currency for your arrival, but often a selection of notes in a suitable hard currency will do a lot of your bargaining for you.

6. THINK AHEAD AND ALLOW YOURSELF FALLBACKS

If you're going to be working during the trip, it's all the more important to ensure that you've anticipated problems. It's not enough to presume that your trusty laptop and its aging internal modem will ensure hassle-free connectivity to your company. Think about how you will establish connections.

» Are you counting on plugging in at a hotel or in a private home? If so, have you checked that you have the appropriate adaptors?
» If your laptop dies, can you resort to your PDA?
» If you are used to relying on a wireless PDA such as a Blueberry or a Palm VII, will it still work abroad? Many wireless devices will not function outside their home country simply because different countries reserve different frequencies for specific purposes, including for the military and police.
» If neither your PC nor your PDA works, will a cybercafé be there to come to the rescue? Find out beforehand (try the cybercafé search engines at www.cybercafe.com or cybercaptive.com).
» Save and back up your work regularly – accidents will happen and they happen a lot more when equipment is being moved around and support is harder to find. Back up to a floppy if need be, or to a remote site if your office or virtual office has hard-drive space you can use. If not, then remember that you can e-mail your day's work to yourself every evening, when it will be safely stored at your e-mail host.

7. DON'T PAY THE FULL RATE AT HOTELS

This has become something of a motto for the more savvy business traveler; and yet many travelers, even those who will spend considerable effort chasing the cheapest airfare, don't even think of trying to drive down a room rate. Discounting and special rates are as much a part of the hotel trade as of the airline business, and it's not just the vast corporations that have enough clout to demand preferential deals. The independent traveler who goes to a particular city frequently will do well to explain that to a hotel and see if they will give a better deal in return for regular use. Your travel agent may be able to negotiate a deal, although the flip side of that coin is that you will often do better to talk to a hotel directly and use your charm, rather than pinning your hopes on an agent's cursory questioning.

Even if you can't get a reduction in rate, you're always better off asking if there's any kind of special offer or if perhaps they could upgrade you a better room. Different hotels in different parts of the world have special offers of which you may never have heard, so it pays to ask – the author once got a particularly good special at the Sohar

Beach Hotel in Oman because it happened to be the holy month of Ramadan.

8. DON'T FORGET TO EARN AND SPEND YOUR AIR MILES

Ever since they were introduced in 1981, the frequent-flyer program and its offspring the Air Mile have become bywords for business travelers, for whom they are often one of the key perks of country-hopping for the company. The fact that the company pays for the ticket but the traveler and family get to enjoy the free flights is one of the more endearing and effective bribes in business. Remembering to claim Air Miles is a must, therefore, as is being aware that they can be earned in more ways than one. Several airlines have experimented with offering extra Air Miles, sometimes double, as an incentive for booking online. Other airlines will throw in free Air Miles if you agree to take an earlier flight, something they do to avoid the need for bumping (see Step 9). Most have partnerships with hotel chains and car rental agencies, all of which can be used to add to your points total.

When it comes to using those points, however, it can be hard to cash them for the day or destination you desire. It has been suggested that if everyone entitled to a free flight on Air Miles were to claim it at once, it could drag many carriers to their knees. Whether or not that is true, the fact remains that there are often draconian limitations imposed on using Air Mile flights. Peak season is usually impossible, and even out of peak you have to remember that any airline reserves only so many seats for Air Mile freebies. It's first come, first served, so it pays to plan ahead. If your first attempt to redeem your Air Miles founders on the rocks of availability, try shifting away from direct flights to those with stopovers. US readers should also note that outside the US very few airlines will allow you to swap Air Miles for an upgrade to a different class.

9. STOPOVERS AND VOLUNTEERING FOR BUMPING

Fancy a night in a decent hotel in a romantic, unfamiliar city on your way to your destination? Curiously enough you can often have one, free of charge, if you arrange a stopover flight. This is where good travel agents come into their own, as those with real industry knowledge will be able to tell you which airlines will automatically put up their passengers if they are flying in on one day but not leaving until a connecting flight the next. For example, the author has enjoyed the occasional day in Amman purely by courtesy of Royal Jordanian Airways, which provided the hotel, transfers, and food for transit passengers (for whom visa requirements were conveniently waived). It doesn't hurt to ask.

The other unexpected bonus can come from offering to be bumped. Involuntary bumping is travel hell. It happens when the airline has overbooked – only an airline could sell you a ticket and then insist you call to reconfirm that you want what you have already paid for and would prefer it not to be sold to someone else. Sometimes, however, overbooking means that there are simply too many passengers for the flight and the sad fact is that preference tends to go to those who have paid the most, however late they show. Voluntary bumping, however, is when you guess that overbooking is a possibility and state that your itinerary is flexible and that you might consider being put on an alternative flight if there is a suitable incentive. Some airlines actively encourage passengers to do this, such as South African through their Flexible Flyer scheme. Incentives can include hotels and entertainment, free or cheap flights, and often straight cash in hand.

10. DON'T FORGET YOUR EXPENSES

Don't laugh! A survey conducted by Visa suggested that some 40% of business people ended up out of pocket on expenses because of items that they forgot to charge, didn't dare to mention, or couldn't find the receipts for. One tip is to use your handheld computer (Palm machines come with an expenses application) or laptop computer (a dedicated spreadsheet will do) to note down expenses every day.

KEY LEARNING POINTS

» Preparation is the key to success. Find out about your destination, the places you need to get to, and the availability of the resources you will need in order to get your work done.
» The arrival is the most stressful and hazardous moment of most trips. Smooth over potential hazards by sorting out beforehand

everything you need and anything you need to know at the airport before you arrive.

» Ensure you have fallbacks in case of common business disasters such as your cards not being accepted, your laptop expiring, or your modem refusing to mate with the local phone plugs.

» Think a little laterally and always try to ask for a better deal, not just on plane upgrades but at your hotel.

» Don't forget to submit your full expenses – nearly half of us end up out of pocket on business trips.

Frequently Asked Questions (FAQs)

Q1: How can the Web help me explore the wide world?

A: See Chapter 4, The E-Dimension.

Q2: Is the Web always the best way of booking trips or holidays?

A: No, but for a consideration of the benefits and drawbacks see the "Best practice" section in Chapter 4.

Q3: Traveler or tourist?

A: Ah, that old chestnut – refer to Chapter 2.

Q4: What advice is there for business travelers planning trips?

A: You can find tips for a perfect Express Exec trip in Chapter 10, Ten Steps to Making Travel Work.

Q5: Where can I find out about the risks and dangers of travel to a particular location?

A: Chapter 5 has a "Best practice" section on the subject.

Q6: How do I maintain a clean conscience about the impact of my travel on the exotic and unspoiled locations I choose to visit?

A: Ecotourism is discussed in Chapter 8, Key Concepts, and success stories of ecotourism are cited in Chapter 7.

Q7: What are the top ten cultural and ecotourist destinations at the moment?

A: Chapter 8, Key Concepts, includes current listings.

Q8: What is retro/sustainable/soft-adventure travel?

A: There are definitions and examples in Chapter 8, Key Concepts.

Q9: Where can I find the best sites offering prices and advice for my next trip?

A: Chapter 9, Resources, includes listings of advice and booking sites for the traveler.

Q10: How do I get online from a foreign country?

A: You can find Internet tips from far-flung foreign locations in Chapter 10.

Index